TANDEM LEADERSHIP

Manager and *Who Moved My Cheese?* Gina Catalano takes a sticky subject—choosing the right second-in-command in your growing business as you transition from solopreneur to true CEO—and walks you through the process of crafting the business and personal life you have always wanted to achieve."

—Sue Rasmussen, coach and international best-selling author of *My Desk Is Driving Me Crazy: End Overwhelm, Do Less, and Accomplish More*

"They say the best things come in small packages, and this is absolutely true with *Tandem Leadership*. This entertaining management fable is a must-read for entrepreneurs to prepare for the inevitable point when they can no longer be solely 'the guy' and need to add a strong #2 to continue on the path to realizing their vision."

—James Walling, CFA, Founding Principal, Accretive Strategies Consulting Group

"While many visionary leaders recognize their need for a right-hand person with complimentary operational leadership skills, too many of these relationships flame out early. In *Tandem Leadership*, Gina Catalano provides a how-to framework for the entrepreneurial and operational leaders to successfully build a business together."

—Steve Straub, Dean of Manufacturing & Agriculture Technologies, Fox Valley Technical College

"Sometimes being at the top can be very lonely in small business. The COO, or "second-in-command" position, is often overlooked but can be essential in freeing up the owner to do what they do best and a partner that provides support in the design process. This book shows how implementing a two-person leadership team can help a business reach its goals and improve its bottom line."

—**Jay Miller**, Principal/Creative Director, Imagehaus

"If you could ask 100 successful leaders the key to their success, chances are they will speak to the strength of their team. Great leaders share responsibility and work. Trusting your #2 allows a leader to focus on the horizon and look for what's next. As Catalano notes in her conclusion, "you don't need to go it alone," and the best leaders never do. *Tandem Leadership* puts forward the power of partnership and provides advice and insights for leveraging your #2."

—**Jennifer McNelly**, Executive Director,
The Manufacturing Institute

"Extremely well written, highlighting the importance of mentorship, and making the most efficient use of your time! A must read for any entrepreneur in the trenches of building a business!"

—**Mycal Anders**, MS, CSCS, Owner,
Next Level Performance & Fitness Consulting

"*Tandem Leadership* is a refreshing and compelling approach for business entrepreneurs that we need to bolster our team with additional business support, e.g. a good #2. As small business owners, invariably, we don't know what we don't know. Being alone, not having the luxury of a stable, experienced team to call on can be daunting. Working 60-70 hours trying to be the head cook and bottle washer is not the answer to successfully moving your business forward and the result often is to second guess yourself.

"Having spent 25+ years in the consulting business working with many small business owners, I know first-hand how hard it is to coach leaders to let go. Tandem Leadership is an easy read written in a novel format, allowing the reader to assimilate the characters in the story and relate to the real world of problem solving. Many years ago I read *The Goal*, a novel-based lean manufacturing book that really helped launch my journey in understanding the power of "Lean" and how it could be implemented in all organizations. *Tandem Leadership* could do the same for your leadership approach."

—**Nigel K. Moore**, President/CEO,
Total Wellness Strategies, LLC

TANDEM
LEADERSHIP
How Your #2 Can Make You #1

Gina Catalano

NEW YORK

NASHVILLE • MELBOURNE • VANCOUVER

TANDEM LEADERSHIP
How Your #2 Can Make You #1

© 2017 **Gina Catalano**

Published in New York, New York, by Morgan James Publishing in partnership with Difference Press. Morgan James is a trademark of Morgan James, LLC. www.MorganJamesPublishing.com

The Morgan James Speakers Group can bring authors to your live event. For more information or to book an event visit The Morgan James Speakers Group at www.TheMorganJamesSpeakersGroup.com.

ISBN 978-1-68350-257-9 paperback
ISBN 978-1-68350-258-6 eBook
ISBN 978-1-68350-259-3 hardcover
Library of Congress Control Number:
2016915904

Cover Design by:
John Weber

Interior Design by:
Bonnie Bushman
The Whole Caboodle Graphic Design

In an effort to support local communities, raise awareness and funds, Morgan James Publishing donates a percentage of all book sales for the life of each book to Habitat for Humanity Peninsula and Greater Williamsburg.

Get involved today! Visit
www.MorganJamesBuilds.com

DEDICATION

For my clients: thank you for sharing your stories, trusting me with your dreams, and letting me join your magic carpet rides. It is an honor.

TABLE OF CONTENTS

INTRODUCTION

"It is good to have an end to journey toward, but it is the journey that matters, in the end."
—Ursula K. LeGuin

Entrepreneurs come to their business in many different ways. But if you ask them, they all have a story.

"I saw this problem and figured out a way to solve it. I couldn't believe no one had thought of it before."

"My dad got sick and my mom asked me to help out. A few months turned into ten years. I can't imagine doing anything else."

"I started making these for some family and friends, and the next thing you know, everyone had to have them. What a roller coaster ride!"

"We were at a reception at the university and this professor told us about his research. As we were leaving, my partner and I looked at each other and knew this technology could be huge. We had to turn it into a business. And we did."

This is the story we hear when they are interviewed for a local newspaper, a trade magazine, a podcast, or when someone politely inquires as to how they started their business. It sounds so simple, so clear and obvious. We want to know how the business started – as if that is the hardest part. But for most of us, it's just a kind of destiny (opportunity + hard work + persistence), which isn't really destiny at all. The idea or the genesis of our business is what makes the headline – but it's the journey that defines us.

Tales of a hero with an improbable task and a journey made possible by the unwavering support of faithful companions – along with the help of a wizard or two throughout the journey – litter the landscape of ancient and modern storytelling. Our hero, challenged, perhaps a little bruised and battered – but ultimately transformed – shows us how the enemy is not outside but within. Because we all have stories, and the struggles are not singular to him alone, the story of Marcus (our hero) and his guide, Bill, growing his company, is constructed as fiction. However, his experience as an entrepreneur and a business owner are not make-believe.

Simultaneously facing immense optimism and self-doubt, the overwhelm of success and fear of failure, impatience and the ability to wait out the big opportunity, Marcus learns these struggles are all part of the gig as the newly minted leader of his fledgling company.

From my experience, the most successful leaders have a keen awareness that they and their businesses can be better, which may be why you are reading this now. They strive for their absolute best and understand the need to thrive while learning throughout all parts of the journey – regardless of how smooth or rough the road may be. They see unsolved problems as opportunities, and remain focused on the challenge until those problems are resolved. They understand the need to be challenged and rise to the next level. They seek out knowledge, and when necessary, accept guidance and accountability from a mentor. Recognizing and excelling at what they do best, they actively seek support to balance their weaknesses. They know they cannot do everything themselves, finding others who complement them. They take risks, make mistakes, but don't let those mistakes define them.

Successful entrepreneurs simply don't stop until they reach their destination. I often think of the journey as climbing through the forest covering a very steep mountain. The higher you climb, the steeper the mountain, and the smaller steps you take. The forest looks the same and there is no indication you are any closer to the top than you were when you started. It starts to feel tedious and unending. Around the time you think you should turn around and go back down the mountain because certainly you've lost your way, the forest thins and the entire valley lies before you. You have reached the summit – and you are so glad you did not waver and turn back. Of course, if you are a typical entrepreneur, it won't take you long to notice there is another, taller, more interesting mountain on the other side of the valley, and you start your next journey.

I have been in love with bicycles since I could remember. Before kindergarten, I taught myself to ride a neighbor's bike on the sly because my parents thought I was too young. I continued to ride like a criminal until, at age seven, I received my purple Schwinn with chrome fenders and saddle baskets. I felt freedom as I never would again (until I received my driver's and motorcycle licenses). I'm a girl who likes to move, which has led me to the entrepreneurial lifestyle – presently, as a leader and a coach. A textbook oldest child, it's not exactly a surprise that for most of my life I have either been the leader or the next in line. Through my own experience in business and life, as well as those of my clients who I have consulted and coached, *Tandem Leadership* was derived.

Tandem Leadership is a model for the relationship between a leader and his #2 person or second-in-command. Two wheels attached to a platform with distinct functions and responsibility to move the organization forward more effectively than the leader could do solo. *Tandem Leadership* will not save a business from the challenges associated with having no products, customers, or cash. But fully implementing *Tandem Leadership* will keep an entrepreneur moving their company forward and improve their chances for success because they can focus their time and talents on being the leader their organization needs. It will reduce the chance of squandering those fleeting opportunities, leveraging scarce resources, and providing a better journey.

Whether you are still riding solo or have an entire team at your side, it is my truest hope that sharing Marcus's story of challenges, redemption, and success will enable and embolden you to use the principles of *Tandem Leadership* to drive your own vision to create the life you are destined to achieve.

CHAPTER 1

My goal was to get into the office early this morning. I had an appointment at 8:00 a.m. and wanted to give myself plenty of time to prepare. Not surprisingly, I was running late. My three-year-old daughter, Cassie, couldn't sleep. I ended up spending much of my night doing the late-night toddler bed shuffle. With our oldest kids, my wife, Maggie, typically had been the one to do this. Maggie often says, "Cassie is a Daddy's girl, and that's fine by me. I did my time with Cole and Daisy."

We had both agreed that if we had the resources, we wanted one of us to stay home with the kids – at least until they were in school. Maggie had the more flexible career, and was definitely better suited than me to be that parent.

She is a school therapist, and still does one day per week as a consultant for the local school district, conducting teacher and staff training. We've known each other since college, though we didn't start dating until we were both in our best friends' wedding – Kyle and Mandy. We've joked since, it's too bad we weren't dating sooner – we could have saved some money and had a double ceremony, as most of the same people came to both weddings.

So, I skipped the gym to get in faster. (I know this is not a great idea – there's a history of heart disease in my family and Maggie is always after me to exercise more and eat healthier.) I grabbed a very large cup of over-caffeinated coffee and raced over to the office. I like getting in early; it gives me time to think. It's getting harder and harder now that we're hiring more people. Kathy, our office manager, likes to get in early as well – but tries to give me a wide berth until I have my coffee.

The truth is, I couldn't sleep last night. Cassie was a welcome distraction. I kept thinking about everything going on, what was in front of me this week, and how everything was going to get done with all this new business coming in. My company makes fixtures for convenience stores. It's actually an innovation – a new way to stack product that provides more room for the product, yet still makes it attractive and easier for the customer to grab. Bottom line is our products optimize minimal shelf space – always a problem for retailers, but especially so for convenience stores.

I got my start in sales, after college, working for a snack foods distribution company, Diamond Bros. Over time, I worked my way up to regional manager. Along the way, I hit it off with Dan Franks, one of the owners of a local chain of convenience stores, Penny's Pantry. He was a little older than me and had just taken over the family business. One day, as we were playing in a golf tournament, Dan shared his frustrations about the business, and an idea came to me the next morning – for a different style of shelf fixture. I had worked in my Uncle Jake's machine shop in high school, so I understood a little how the new fixtures could be made. Jake helped me figure out how to make them, and with some testing in Dan's stores, I knew we had a viable product that could be really successful. I wasn't quite ready to quit the security and the life of my current job. Let's face it – by then, I had been there 13 years and worked myself into a pretty good gig. It wasn't always easy, but I knew what needed to be done, and was well-compensated for my efforts. Yet, I was getting a little bored, and there was even talk we were going to be bought out by a larger competitor. They already had a sales network in the area, and everyone knows what happens to the acquired sales team when the deal is done.

That was two years ago. Since then, my Aunt Molly got cancer (Uncle Jake's wife) and beat it. Jake wasn't young at the time – almost 65 – but anyone who knew him would have placed a bet he would be the last person to actually retire. But Molly's illness scared him, and they both decided they were ready to do more of the travelling they had been putting off for the "someday" in their future.

Diamond Bros was bought out. Though I was offered a position to stay with the new company, I was ready for something else. I took the buyout coming as part of the sale. Jake approached me about buying his machine shop as a platform for starting my new business. Turns out Jake's real talent was investing in the stock market. Molly and Jake had always lived so frugally that I was shocked to learn they had more than enough to retire well. They had no children of their own, and had always been exceptionally generous to me and my sister. His repayment terms were excellent. So while I was very touched by his offer, it really wasn't that surprising. Everything was lining up, and I just couldn't say no.

So, Shelfwerx was born – about nine months ago. I inherited five of Jake's employees: four machine operators and Kathy. Our first customer for the new business, of course, was Dan's chain of stores. Through some trial and error, we were able to figure out how to design several different kinds of fixtures to build our line. Everyone was pretty happy, though it took much longer than any of us anticipated. We are on track to break $1M this year in sales for new business.

I knew my experience and relationships in the industry would be the keys to our success, and I was anxious to get to the big industry trade shows to start promoting Shelfwerx. But the problems in the shop kept getting in the way: a week turned into a month, and then it was three months later. Finally, I hired a supervisor for the shop. He brought two guys with him. There was so much opportunity out there to sell, but I could never get out of the shop. Finally, last month, I was able to attend one of the smaller trade shows where I had the opportunity to pitch Shelfwerx to a regional drugstore chain, Quick Drugstores.

Two weeks ago, an email arrived in my inbox:

Marcus:

I've been able to sell Shelfwerx to our internal team and we would like to do a test in our concept store for our candy assortment aisles. Obviously, there are details to work out but if this works, we'd like to roll out in all of our stores and perhaps look at other product assortments to use the Shelfwerx product.

Please contact me to discuss the details on becoming a qualified vendor and project details. We have a short timeline – we'd like to have this in place for the holiday season.

Vaughn Tappan
VP, Operations
Quick Drugstores

At first, I yelled. Kathy, who sits next door, came by to see what was going on. After I told her, I was surprised at her reaction. "What's going on, Kathy?" Kathy was a straight shooter who knew how to be direct after years of working in the machining business.

"Look, I know this is a great thing, but look around: I already have piles of things you've been promising to take care of. *For weeks.* How do you think anything is going to get done if you're tied up all the time with new customers? The CPA said you have to meet with him by next week to review the quarterly taxes, our lease needs to be renegotiated, and you wanted the website up last week. Jake's looking for the monthly financials and he said you two discussed having monthly board meetings. Maggie called this morning to tell me to remind you that you agreed to coach Cole's baseball team, which starts next week." Kathy stopped for a moment. "Marcus, don't get me wrong. I really like being here and working for you, but you've been so caught up in getting the shop turned around and getting Dan's stores up to speed, that it feels like everything else here has just stalled. We need more help. You need help – and fast. I'm doing what I can, but some of this stuff is just outside of my comfort zone."

"Kathy, we'll figure it out. We always do, right?" I gave her my best "can do" attitude and started looking through the stack of papers she had been holding for me. The more I started sorting through everything, I knew Kathy was right. And all of a sudden the email from Vaughn Tappan seemed like an anchor around my neck. Companies are supposed to grow, right? How was this going to work? What kind of help? Did we even have the resources to hire someone? We had done budgets, but not for the kind of growth Vaughn discussed in his email. And frankly, even though I had colleagues at my previous job, it was basically me and the entry level sales guys. I didn't have a lot of experience really running a business from every angle. I believed in the product – and the response we were getting from the industry was phenomenal – but for the first time, I realized my company could be in trouble. It never occurred to me too many sales were going to be a bad thing.

A week later, Jake called and asked to meet for lunch. He and Molly were preparing for a once-in-a -lifetime adventure of sailing around the world for three months. I drove downtown to Jerry's Top Town Diner. My grandparents used to take Jake and my mom there as kids and Maggie and I did the same with

Cassie, Daisy, and Cole. The waitresses called you "hon" and still wore those white dresses with black aprons and little hats – and they served the best burgers and fries in town. The place was packed, but Jake had arrived early and grabbed us a table in the back. I knew by Jake's tone that our lunch meeting wasn't an optional activity. And by his choosing a table instead of sitting up at the counter, where he could shoot the breeze with the staff, I knew Jake Johnson had something to say – *to me.*

After ordering, Jake didn't waste any time. "So, what's going on at Shelfwerx these days?"

He must have spoken to Kathy. I was angry. She worked for me, now – and not Jake. *How I can I trust her with anything if she's going to run to Jake every time we run up against a few problems?* My face must have showed my anger, because before I could answer, Jake said, "Don't be angry with Kathy. You know Kathy and Molly are close and she stopped by to drop off some things for the trip. She's worried, and frankly, so am I. Shelfwerx has huge potential or else I wouldn't have done what I did. It's not just because you're my nephew that I decided to sell the shop to you."

"Jake, I would never let you down – you know that, right?" It was true. I would do anything to make sure everything was right between us.

"I'm not worried about you letting me down. I'm worried about you letting yourself down and everyone else who is depending on you." He paused. "In my mind, when you become an owner, it's not just about the personal rewards the benefits bring you – it's about all the people who depend on your business – your customers, your employees, the community – everyone is counting on you to make good decisions and be the leader they need to be successful. Sometimes you need help to do it, and you shouldn't be too proud to ask for help."

Before I could ask or respond, the waitress arrived, and we ordered our lunch.

"I'm not sure I understand. I mean, I get what you mean about being responsible to the business, but I'm not afraid to ask for help. Didn't I come to you first when I needed to make the prototypes and the first products for Shelfwerx?" I was confused, and starting to get defensive and angry.

"You did," he went on, "but when I agreed to sell you the shop, do you remember what I told you I needed from you? In addition to paying off the loan, of course."

He let me think a minute. We signed the loan papers at the attorney's office, and both families went out to dinner to celebrate. And then I remembered Jake's toast at dinner, "Nephew, Molly and I are thrilled my little business is going to live on through your new one. We know Shelfwerx is going to be a huge success and we are happy to be a part of it. Cheers!"

He then leaned over to me and said, in a quieter tone, "I believe in you, Marcus. Good or bad – no matter how crazy things get – I always want to know what's going on. It's the one requirement I have. As your investor, you owe me that. Agreed?"

I had nodded my head and promised, "Of course, Jake."

At lunch, I realized I had broken my promise. "I'm sorry, Jake. I've been so busy...."

Jake cut me off. "Marcus, because you are so busy is the exact reason I want to know what's going on. I think the Quick Drugstores deal is great, but I also know you can barely keep your head above water as it is. You work hard, and your business has great potential, but that's just not enough to be a success. The world is full of companies that could have been something and didn't get there. Shelfwerx doesn't need to be one of those companies. You need help, and you need it now."

"Are you offering to work with me?" I was confused.

"I thought about it, Marcus, I really have. If Molly and I weren't going on this trip, I would be rolling up my sleeves and coming over to work with you. Since I can't do that, I've got someone who can do that for me. Let's just say it's my peace of mind about my investment while I'm gone. Bill McEntire and I go back a long time. He's the perfect guy for you. I spoke with him yesterday, and he'll be at your office on Monday at 8:00 a.m."

We talked about Jake's trip, and he asked me about Maggie and the kids, as we finished our lunches. I was still a little angry when I headed back to the office, but I could only blame myself. I had been lax on keeping up my communication with Jake. I knew this trip was important to both Jake and Molly. If it made Jake sleep easier while he was gone, I could work with Bill. I was tired, too. It's not like I didn't want the help – everything had just been happening so fast, I just hadn't had time to work it all out.

So this morning, I was meeting Bill McEntire for the first time – and I was running late. I pulled into the parking lot, and, noticing there were only employee cars, breathed a sigh of relief.

I went to my office and started reading my email. My office overlooked the parking lot, and I would easily notice when he arrived. Soon 30 minutes had passed, and no Bill McEntire. I went out to find Kathy and see if he had called for me.

"Oh, Bill," she said. "He's been here since 7:30. He's out in the shop."

I walked into the warehouse and saw our supervisor, Neil, talking with someone I didn't recognize. I was surprised. Jake had told me a little about Bill McEntire's background. He had gone to school as an engineer, and then decided to go to law school. He never actually practiced law because he came back to run the family business when his father became ill. He was known as a savvy business person – especially in turnarounds. The man talking to Neil was small in stature, and easily in his 70s. But that's not what made him stand out. He was wearing a bicycle helmet – and had one leg of his pant tucked in his left sock, as if he had just hopped off of a bicycle.

Neil saw me come up, "Here's the boss now. Great to meet you, Bill. Thanks for the tips."

"You must be Marcus," Bill said. We shook hands. "I got here a little early and decided to take a look around. Always nice to know what I'm getting into."

"I would have been happy to give you the tour myself," I said, as I wondered what tips he was giving my employees.

"I'm sure we'll have plenty of time to do that." He took off his helmet and walked over to where his bicycle was parked. He looped his helmet over the handle bars, and grabbed a small notebook from his bike pack. "Should we go to your office and have a chat?"

I led him to my office. After getting settled in, he asked, "Tell me about Shelfwerx. Start at the beginning."

I spent the next four hours talking to Bill about everything related to the business: from my time at Diamond Bros, to developing the new products, to starting Shelfwerx. He asked me about Maggie and my family, what I did in my spare time, and what I enjoyed doing as a kid. I talked to him about things I hadn't thought about in years. I wasn't quite clear on why so much information was important, but I thought of Jake and his trust in this guy, and let it go.

And then he asked me to name five things I did yesterday. My answer was:

- Updated the website shopping cart
- Talked to our accountant about changing payroll providers
- Signed checks
- Called the bank about our credit line renewal application status
- Worked on a delivery problem

Finally, he peered over his glasses at me, "Marcus, I want you to take a minute. Tell me, when you think of yourself and Shelfwerx in five years, what do you see?"

I took more than a minute, but it was clear. "I see this company changing the industry. Making it easier for store owners to shelve their products and be more profitable. I see my employees coming to work each day excited to be here, because they are making contributions and getting rewarded for it. I see the company quite a bit bigger and very profitable – our margins are great."

"What's the one thing you did yesterday that is going to get Shelfwerx to your five-year goal?"

My stomach became queasy. "Nothing – not one damn thing."

Bill smiled. "Exactly!"

He must have known how I was feeling because he went on, "This isn't fatal, Marcus. In fact, I think we are starting just in time. But I think we're done for today. Let's meet again next Monday, same time?"

I nodded.

"Great! Your homework for this week is to keep a list of what you do each day. Email me at end of each day. Nothing fancy, just bullet points are fine. Here's my email address: tandemwheels@gmail.com."

He pulled out his smart phone and marked the appointment. He saw me smile, and chuckled. "Thought I was a dinosaur when you saw me ride in on a bicycle? There's a difference between *having* to do something and *wanting* to do something. I'll show myself out. Have a good week."

Bill sure was a character. I wasn't quite certain what had happened in the past four hours, but I somehow felt a little lighter than when I started my day – which was worth something these days. And then a thought occurred to me: We never talked about his fees. What was this going to cost me?

* * *

- What keeps you up at night?
- What is the vision for your life and your business?
- How much of your day is spent fulfilling that vision?

CHAPTER 2

The week went quickly. Quick Drugstores was pushing for the delivery in their demo store, but they kept changing the specs. An inch or two here and there probably didn't sound like a big deal to their merchandising team, but for us – with interlocking parts – it was a nightmare. I kept telling Neil and his team to be patient; it would all be worth it in the end. On top of the back and forth on the design, a bout of the flu hit the company, and almost everyone (including me) was out for at least one day. I did as Bill had asked, and emailed him a list of the tasks I had done each day. Some days I felt like I hadn't accomplished much, and was a little embarrassed by what I sent him.

On Thursday, Jake called. He and Molly were leaving on Friday, and he wanted to check in. We talked about the trip, and he asked me if I needed anything from him before he left. I reassured him everything was going well, and that Bill and I were working together.

"Marcus, don't let Bill fool you," he said. "He may have some peculiar characteristics, but he knows what he's doing. You're in good hands."

I told him I would email him if anything came up, and he said he'd call when they were in port. "Jake, don't worry about anything here. You and Molly deserve this trip. I want you to have a good time."

While I had been emailing Bill all week, I had only received a simple, "Received - Regards, Bill" after each email submission. I wondered what he was doing with all this information. However, on Friday afternoon, I received the following email:

Marcus:

For Monday, please review your list and do the following:

Top 5 most favorite things I like to do

Top 5 least favorite things I like to do

Regards,

Bill

I looked through my list. It was long and full of a lot of things I didn't like to do. Who likes to evaluate payroll vendors, sign checks, or select phone systems? But then I noticed I was having an equally difficult time selecting my top five favorites as well. Finally, I settled on each of my five and put my list away for the weekend.

On Monday, Bill arrived, as usual via bicycle. While I was waiting for Bill, I decided to go out into the warehouse and work with Neil on the week's schedule. We were scheduled to deliver the Quick Drugstores prototypes in a few weeks, and we still were having some problems with the fixtures. Neil had some good ideas on how to fix the problem, and he said he'd keep me posted. As I spied Bill coming in the door, Neil asked, "By the way, have you thought about how you want this packaged?"

I looked at him, "What do you mean?"

"Well, with the Penny's Pantry jobs, after the first store, we just brought the stuff over to the distribution center and their guys put everything together. How are we delivering this set-up to Quick Drugstores?"

Now Bill had overheard the entire conversation, and I was stumped. Because Dan and I had worked on the product together, there wasn't a formal delivery or installation process. They were okay with receiving the product in parts, as their internal maintenance team took care of everything. This was one more thing to add to my list for the week. "Let me check with Quick Drugstores and I'll get back to you before the end of the week."

"So, Marcus," Bill asked as we settled into my office. "Tell me about your list. What did you see?"

I took a deep breath. "What I noticed is I do a lot of things I don't like to do. But someone has to do them, right? Isn't that part of paying my dues?"

Bill ignored my question. "What are your five favorite things from last week?"

I reviewed my list. "Working with Quick Drugstores on their design questions, troubleshooting the fixture issue for Quick Drugstores with our team, looking at the attendee list for the next Trade Show and evaluating prospects, discussing some different cash management strategies with our CPA, and checking in with Penny's Pantry on their next order."

"And your least favorite?"

"Signing checks, payroll vendor selection, employee health insurance review, dealing with two employees who aren't getting along, and answering a false alarm at the building."

"So, when you look at your two lists," he asked. "What do you notice?"

I looked at them again. The things I didn't like to do were the day-to-day mechanics of running the company, while the things I liked to do were the customer and product tasks. My favorites list also represented the things I was good at. I looked up at Bill, and he was smiling. I shared my observations between the two lists.

"Interesting, isn't it? Where we focus our time and energy is where we are going to get our results. By looking at your list, I'd say you're well on your way to making an excellent office manager."

I should have been offended, but he made sense. He continued, "By nature, we humans are creatures of habit. In fact, our brain is wired for habits – good or bad – and it will continue to find the quickest path so we don't have to think about what we're doing. What was painful or annoying slowly just becomes something we don't consider or evaluate."

"Like the frog story: the one where he starts out in cold water, and even though the temperature is only turned up one degree at a time, he stays in until he's boiling and it's too late," I laughed. "I definitely don't want to be served up as cooked frog legs down at Chateau La Mer."

"No, you don't. The first step in moving forward is having a good understanding of where you are and where you want to be. When I asked you last week what your vision is for yourself and Shelfwerx five years from now, you were able to articulate that to me. But what I wanted you to notice is that your desire to get there isn't matching what you are actually doing. Your vision or your intent should drive your actions. Do you see that now?" he asked.

"Yes, I do," I sighed. "But I'm not sure what I need to do next. Everyone around here is pretty tapped out. I can't imagine dumping everything I'm doing on Kathy or Neil. I'm not sure we can afford to just hire someone at this moment. Are you suggesting I consider taking on a partner?"

"Do you think you need a partner?" he asked.

"Well, it would be great to have someone to split up some of the risk. You know, have some skin in the game. Having another person invested in the business as much as I am, and willing to work as hard as me, and perhaps bring in some more talent and cash," I mused. "It would nice not to be the only one here at night when I'm trying to get my real work done."

Bill thought for a minute, "Do you think there could be anyone as invested in Shelfwerx as you are right now?"

"No, I guess, not really." I slumped in my chair. "It was my idea, and I know what the product means to my customers and its potential. I mean, I have so many ideas on how to extend the product, now that I know how it's working. I'm sure we can stay ahead of any competitors who try and design their own version of our products."

"Most of the time, when someone says to me they want a partner, they don't really want a partner. They have some worry or fear about failing, or not being smart or talented enough, perhaps in the areas they are least familiar with in their business. So, it seems logical if they find someone who has the complementary skills as a partner, everything will balance out." He continued, "What I've found when someone says they want a partner, what they really want is support, resources, and risk reduction. And you don't need a partner to acquire those."

Bill got up to get some coffee. When he came back, he suggested we take a walk around the block to stretch our legs and "get the blood flowing." Bill was probably at least a half a foot shorter than I was, and twice my age, but he walked so quickly that I found myself quickening my pace to keep up with him. Then he would slow down, and I found myself going much slower than I normally walked … and being somewhat distracted to what he was saying, because I was worried we were going to run into each other.

When we returned to my office, he asked, "How comfortable were you in walking with me at my pace?"

"Which one?" We both laughed. "I found it sometimes faster, sometimes slower than my normal walking speed.

Honestly, I thought I was going to keep bumping into you at the end."

"We started at the exact same place, but have completely different gaits. You can match someone step for step for a while, but it becomes exhausting in the process. Eventually, one person will be ahead and the other behind. You may change positions, for example, if one person needs to stop – but it's rare both people can keep up at the *exact* same pace for any length of time. That's one of the reasons I think it's difficult for most business partnerships to be successful for any length of time. As much as we say we're fine with someone being ahead or behind us, as entrepreneurs it's a frustrating experience. Do you know what a Sherpa is?"

"Sure, they help mountain climbers in the Himalayas."

"Well, when I say someone who says they are looking for a partner is really looking for support, resources, and risk reduction, I think of the mountain climber and the Sherpa. When serious mountain climbers attempt to trek Mount Everest, they employ Sherpas as guides. The mountain climber provides the desire and vision (to get to the top). The Sherpas provide support (carrying supplies and making camp), resources (directions, tips, suggestions), and risk reduction (knowledge of the trail, impact of the atmosphere on the climber, etc.). And as much as the Sherpas do, in the end, it's up to the mountain climber to climb the mountain. He might not be able to climb the mountain by himself, but the Sherpas also can't climb the mountain *for* him. Just as entrepreneurs, as much as we want to have someone sharing our business journey, it is really our journey to complete."

"So, what you're saying is, I really need a Sherpa to help me carry my load up the mountain," I laughed.

"Something like that," he replied. "This week, I'd like you to make your list as you did last week. But at the end of each day, review your list and separate them this way: tasks that can be done only by you, tasks someone currently employed at Shelfwerx could do if they had the time, and tasks you would need to find another resource for."

I told him I would divide up my list and send him an update at the end of the week.

- How much of your day is spent working on tasks you "want" to do compared to tasks you feel you "have" to do?
- What are your greatest challenges?
- What tasks or jobs do you currently do that someone else could do?

CHAPTER 3

After Bill left, I contacted Vaughn Tappan at Quick Drugstores to discuss Neil's question about delivery and installation. I suggested our team oversee this first installation, to make sure everything went smoothly. I realized "our" team would most likely mean me and Neil, and I added another thing to my list for Bill to review the following week.

On Tuesday, I met with Gary Montgomery. He had called and offered to buy me lunch if he could get some advice on networking and ideas for a new job. Gary managed distribution for Diamond Bros, and had also been offered a job with the new company. Unlike me, he had chosen to stay on. After nine months, he was struggling with the company culture, and he was looking for something new. I understood how he felt. The year leading up to the buyout, the family that owned Diamond Bros had brought in a new team to prepare the company for sale. The informal nature of the company had changed quite a bit then, and for some us more entrepreneurial types, the atmosphere had become more than a little suffocating.

I had always liked Gary. He had been my "go to" guy when one of my customers was having problems with their deliveries. During our lunch, the more he talked, the more excited I became. He was looking for the exact kind of opportunity I had realized I needed just the day before. He had experience I didn't know about, which I thought we needed. It took everything I had to not offer him the job right then. But with Jake being out of town, I thought I would run my thoughts about my conversation with Gary past Bill in our next meeting.

During the week, I found myself looking at my "Bill List" differently. Every time I evaluated a task I didn't want to do, or thought I should do in the future, I thought of Kathy, Neil, and even Gary. I was worried about overloading Kathy and Neil – they both seemed as busy as or even busier than me – and I wondered how they would feel about the extra work. On Thursday, Kathy stopped by my office.

"I was wondering if you had a chance to review the payroll vendor recommendations Hunter Jackson sent over?" she asked. Hunter Jackson was our CPA firm.

"I'm sorry. I haven't had a chance," I answered. Her face fell. "What's wrong, Kathy?"

"I was hoping we could get everything taken care of before the quarter ends," she went on, "The current way I have to manage the guys' timeclock data is a pain. Really, they might as well be handing me their time on sticky notes for what good it is. The way ChexNow! does its data conversion is amazing. I think it might eliminate at least two or three hours a week of bookkeeping work for me, and save a couple hours a quarter for Hunter Jackson in reconciling everything."

"I knew it was a problem for you, but I didn't realize how much." I promised to look through the proposals before the end of the day.

After lunch, I pulled up the email Kathy had forwarded to me from Hunter Jackson to review. What I hadn't noticed, when I first received the email, was that Kathy had also provided a quick analysis of what her preference of the two providers would be, based on how much time she thought it would save us and our CPA firm. She also included the following note:

> *Marcus:*
>
> *I really like ChexNow! I did a quick phone call to some people I know who have used both ChexNow! and PayrollEZ. PayrollEZ seems a little better deal, but what I heard is that ChexNow! is more compatible with different business software programs, and easier to use. I was also told that they have better customer training and support. They are located in Smithville, and offer a local users group to get customer feedback. Let me know if you need any more information.*
>
> *Kathy*

I looked through the information the CPA firm put together, and they recommended either vendor. ChexNow! was slightly more expensive, but the cost savings coming from the items Kathy noted would mean it would more than pay for itself. And, it would free Kathy up to do a few more things for me. I emailed my decision to her and Hunter Jackson. *One more thing off my list,* I thought to myself as I went to coach Cole's baseball team.

The athletic complex was on the other side of town. It was an amazing facility: a far cry from what I was used to from my early days playing baseball in this very same program. There were all new fields for both baseball and soccer, and an all-purpose indoor facility used for community recreation and education programs. The nature preserve lined one side, and the high school on the other connected with the town's biking and walking trails. For once, I was early as I waited for Erik Lindstrom, the other coach, and the rest of the team to arrive. I sat on the bleachers at our assigned practice field checking my email on my phone when I heard someone come up off the bike path.

"Marcus, is that you?" I looked up and it was Bill. He grinned, "Playing hooky today?"

I stumbled like a school kid being caught by the principal, which made Bill laugh out loud, "I'm just kidding with you. Glad to see you have your priorities straight! I'm assuming one of your kids is playing here today?"

"Cole – my oldest – he's 10. I help coach his team."

"Good for you," he leaned his bicycle against the backstop. "Baseball is a great sport. I hear from Jake you were quite the player in your day."

"State champs my junior year," I paused. "It was a great time. I loved playing. And winning the way we did, it was great. There's something about cut grass on a warm day that brings me back to that time."

"I know what you mean. I might just sit and watch for a while, Coach."

Bill proceeded to grab a seat at the top of the bleachers. I wanted to tell him about my lunch with Gary, but Erik, the other coach, and his son arrived – along with Cole and some of the other players and their parents. Soon after, we were getting the kids divided onto the field in their practice groups, and I was preoccupied with keeping their attention. All of our players had experience, and our league prided itself on the caliber of instruction and quality of competition it provided for its traveling teams. I looked up to the bleachers several times, and saw Bill watching the practice intently. He even had his little notebook and was scribbling some notes. After practice was over, I came out of the dugout – but Bill was gone.

On Monday morning, I told Bill about my lunch with Gary, expressed he might be the missing piece to our operation, and asked for his thoughts.

Bill asked me a question. "What position did you play in high school?"

"Catcher, mainly. I was a pretty solid hitter, so I always played because they needed my bat," I went on. "I liked catching, though, because you can see the whole field, and you are always in play."

"I noticed at your practice you move the kids around to all the positions."

"Yeah, even at this age, the kids want to focus on one position – or maybe it's their parents who push them to specialize. But so many of them are undeveloped yet, and we work to get them as much exposure to the different positions as possible," I laughed. "Plus, they all want to be pitchers!"

"Baseball is interesting," he went on. "You get a glove and a ball, and you can throw the ball in the air and catch it yourself. You add a second person, and you're playing catch. You add a third person, and you have a batter, and so on."

"We had a group of about nine or ten of us playing street ball when I was growing up," I continued his thought process. "We had enough players to have fun."

"Here's the deal. Regardless if you had 18 players for two full teams, or 10 players for a "street" game, you're still playing ball, right?" He went on. "In street ball, the pitcher might have to cover first base while the two outfielders cover second and third base. When you have a complete team, like your championship high school team, a pitcher may back up first base or a shortstop will take second or third, but they all have a primary responsibility first. They are specialists."

He waited a minute to see if I was following him. "If you look at your Shelfwerx team, what kind of ball are you playing?"

I thought a minute, "We're playing street ball, but we're really in the majors now. Quick Drugstores is just the beginning, I think. There a lot of other stores out there that could use our product. Wait – I mean, *need* our product. Our shelving is like no other on the market right now – with the limited space and tight margins, Shelfwerx does an awesome job in helping our customers be more profitable. And here we are, running around covering all these positions. It's killing us, really, keeping us from making a dent in the market."

"And like you said – playing street ball is fun. What was the difference in the fun between your street ball games and your championship team?"

"Playing street ball was relaxing fun, but competitive. No adults involved, and sometimes we changed the rules to do crazy stuff, like bat with our eyes closed, or hit from all the bases," I answered. "Our high school team was like a well-oiled machine. We only lost two games, and everyone was really good at their designated positions. It was a different kind of fun – like being so good made us want to work that much harder. *Winning* made it fun."

"And Marcus, you do want to win?"

"Yes, I do – there's nothing like it." I remembered the championship weekend at the state capitol, being interviewed by the local TV station, and getting to ride in a float with my teammates in the Fourth of July parade. "So I need a full team – but how do we add that many more people? We can't afford to have so many specialists right now for each job around here. We're not that big."

"Adding more people to your team is just like fielding your high school championship team. You need to figure out who your players are (including you), and what are their skills and strengths. Where can they excel, and where can they "cover"?

You keep playing modified street ball until you can get your championship team developed," he said. "And by modified street ball, I mean be strategic about how you cover your field. If you only have five players, you don't go chasing every foul ball – you'll be too tired."

Bill left to make a quick call. What he said made sense. I did feel like I was running from behind home plate covering all the bases right now. I'm sure Kathy and Neil felt the same way. Suddenly, I felt as if I were looking down at my business and seeing it for the first time. I could see the guys in the back working away – Kathy and Neil – fielding calls and answering questions. Lately, they were always leaving at the end of the day with more to do than they started. I looked around at my office. I liked organization, but there were too many neat stacks of paper. My To-Do List laid out so nicely on the whiteboard, because I thought it would keep me focused. It hadn't been updated in weeks. We were scrappy and lean, and we were playing with enthusiasm – but were we playing to win? I was competitive by nature, but over the last few years at Diamond Bros, it had become easy for me to hit my targets – and I had done so out of habit, not by passion. That lack of passion in my previous job helped energize me to start my company. But the way I had been working, so far, wasn't going to serve me moving forward.

When Bill came back, I told him: "I want Shelfwerx to be a championship team. Where do I start?"

Bill smiled, "I was hoping you'd say that. Let's take a look at your list from last week."

For the next hour, we plowed through my notes on my tasks. Bill erased my white board. "You're going to have a completely different To-Do List after today," as he put four categories on the board: Customers, Products, Cash, and Infrastructure. I then put every item from my previous week list under one of each of the segments as Bill had instructed me last week. The grid looked something like this:

	Only I Can Do	Current Shelfwerx Only	Outside Shelfwerx Resource
Customers			
Product			
Cash			
Infrastructure			

Bill grilled me each time: "Is it true – are you the only person who can do this task?"

We then went through the list again, and we discussed what items I liked to do, what things I was good at, and what I wanted to do going forward. When we were done, my top three items/categories were:

Getting new business and closing deals
New product ideas
Cash management

I don't love accounting, but I understood – and Bill insisted – that as the owner and without a full-time financial person, I had to keep an eye on the money. Even I had heard of too many horror stories of fraud and embezzlement at companies of all sizes. There was no trust fund to bail me out if I messed this up.

"These are the money makers, Marcus. And they just so happen to be your sweet spot. Are other problems or issues going to come up? Absolutely!" Bill turned back to face me: "But every single day, this is where your focus needs to be – without fail."

We then looked at the remaining items on my list and separated them into current and future functions within the company. I promised I would work with Neil and Kathy over the next week to do the same exercise with them. We also decided to bring Gary in for an interview at the end of the following week. "By then, you'll know exactly what you want him to do and there's less of a chance of hiring the right person for the wrong job."

As he was leaving, he said, "And if you get a chance, brush up on your bicycle riding skills. They'll come in handy next week."

- How much time daily do you spend thinking about and working on strategy?
- How often do you feel like you are scrambling to "just keep up?"
- Do you know what your business "money makers" are?
- How often are you distracted with "foul balls?"

CHAPTER 4

Working with Neil and Kathy to go through their lists was a little tougher. I had wanted to review them together, because I thought it would be helpful for all three of us to know what the other was doing. But logistically, it proved impossible to coordinate that discussion on such short notice. Both Neil and Kathy had after-hours commitments that week, so we settled on one at a time. Because Kathy answered the phones, at her suggestion, we both came in a little earlier one day and reviewed her list – while Neil volunteered to answer the phone until we were done. Neil and I worked together later in the day, and by Friday, I had all three of our lists put together just as Bill and I had done with my list on Monday. My walls were covered with sticky notes, questions, and reminders.

I looked at the entirety of what was going on (or not going on) at Shelfwerx, and felt both concerned and optimistic. We were hitting our schedule for production on the units for the Quick Drugstores demo store, but had just received some complaints from Penny's Pantry about some issues they were having. Because Penny's Pantry did their own installation, and knew Neil from the first few installs, their merchandiser contacted him directly late in the day. Hoping it was a minor issue, Neil had stopped by on his way into work and taken care of the problem for them on-site.

Unknown to Neil, I was scheduled to play in a golf tournament with some of the Penny's Pantry team that very same day. Needless to say, I was surprised to hear about the problem for the first time at the golf tournament. I was embarrassed, and then angry, as I didn't know what was going on in my own company. In the Shelfwerx side of the business, we only had two customers and eight employees! Of course, Neil felt bad when I talked to him about it the next day. We both agreed we could do better, and moved on. I couldn't help but hear Bill in my head talking about chasing foul balls. We needed both focus and more resources.

On Monday, Bill and I reviewed the data I had collected. I had taken what everyone was doing and put it under functions, and then sorted by who was currently responsible for it. It was obvious we had a few holes to fill on our team. I told Bill what had happened the previous week with Neil and Penny's Pantry, and my concerns about keeping everything moving. He asked what I thought could have been done differently.

"I feel like Neil should have known to let me know – even if it was minor," I said. "He said he wanted to get a better understanding of the problem before he 'bothered' me about it, because I have a lot of my plate."

"Interesting," Bill answered, "that he was concerned about how much you have to do. Looking at these lists, Neil seems to have a lot of his own things to do, and not much to do with the customer on a regular basis. If Neil had told you about the problem, would you have handled it any differently?"

"No, probably not," I admitted. "I guess I was just embarrassed in front of the Penny's Pantry guys, which made me angry."

"From my experience, Marcus – having employees be willing to do what Neil did – well, it's something you just can't teach," he answered. "You can fix the communication part with a good game plan, and the right #2."

"By #2, do you mean a COO?" I asked. Diamond Bros had brought in a COO the last year that I was there, in preparation for the sale. His arrival was not met with a lot of enthusiasm by my boss, or any of the other VPs. Granted, many of them had been there a long time, and most had worked up to their position from an entry level position. It just seemed a little too much "C" for the size of our company.

"Possibly," he said, then asked me: "I notice you don't have a title on your business card. Aren't you the CEO and Founder?"

"Yes, I am. My business card is a trick I learned from a couple of my old customers," I told him. "When I used to call on some of my customers at Diamond Bros, one or two didn't have titles on their cards, and I asked them why. They told me they wore a lot of hats and sometimes they wanted a little more flexibility in how they presented themselves, or the ability to be anonymous at a trade show, for example. They might want to be 'just the sales guy' or 'plant manager' sometimes, and other times, the owner. That's also something I learned early in my career calling on smaller, family businesses. I needed to be careful of a tendency to assume who the owner was and who had influence. That nice little old lady receptionist could be the President's mother!"

"So it's not important what the title is, right?" Bill went on. "A good #2, or Second-In-Command, to use a military term, is the key person who helps the CEO, President, Owner of the operation get traction. In a healthy, growing business, the #2 is very strong. Perhaps even better at many things than the CEO. Quite frankly, many of us entrepreneurs have a tendency to run people over with our ideas and methods. If it's the right person, the title won't matter. And in a company like Shelfwerx, the title probably shouldn't matter to whomever you hire as your #2. Does that make sense?"

I nodded. "It does – I never thought about it that way. In a lot of ways, Kathy did a lot of #2 work for Jake when she worked for him as Office Manager. She kept Jake and the shop supervisor hopping."

"Well, we know you need another position: a strong #2 who will support you and the company while you focus on new products and sales," I nodded. Then he went on, "We also both agree that neither Kathy nor Neil is that person?"

"No, they aren't," I answered. "I thought Neil might have been, but I realize now he'd rather 'do' things, and not so much think about coordinating operations on a bigger scale. He's great in the shop, and he did do a great job servicing Penny's Pantry. I guess it's the 'big picture' piece that's missing."

"That's why I asked you to work with them last week in combining your task lists. It's easy to overlook someone internal sometimes, because we like to look at what's shiny and new. But if you have a good employee, and they are ready, moving them up the ladder can be a great thing for the company." He pulled out a piece of paper. "Read through these four descriptions, and tell me which one seems like you the most."

A. Worked his/her way up in the company to get to his/her position. Values the "on-the-job" training and experience. Knows a lot of inside information about the company and/or industry by virtue of the time in the company. (Trainee or Lifer)

B. Supreme troubleshooter and able to fix anything. Likes challenges and is rewarded by new positions or moves onto new jobs very successfully. Enjoys working with others to make changes. (Consultant or Fixer)

C. More ideas than time to implement because his/her ideas are so good. Interested in learning how others are successful and wants to emulate even if following their own path. Able to make decisions without others' input. (Entrepreneur)

D. Routinely found at the top of their chosen field or profession because of their experience and high competency. More concerned with getting things done than having the spotlight. Likes troubleshooting as part of making processes more efficient. (Professional)

"Probably C and a little B," I answered.

"Where do you see your friend Gary on this list?" Bill then asked.

I looked at the list again. "Gary is more of a D with some B, too. He was probably one of the most respected guys at Diamond Bros while I was there."

"That's what I was hoping," Bill said looking at his watch. "Why don't we take a quick break and meet me out in the parking lot in ten minutes. I've got something to show you."

I checked my email and then went to meet Bill in the parking lot. I couldn't believe what I was seeing: Bill was riding a unicycle around the parking lot. He was more than proficient – he was doing figure eights and riding backwards. He saw me come out of the building, and rode up to an SUV with a bike rack and a standard bicycle attached to it.

"Well," he hopped off the unicycle. "Would you like to give this a try?"

I laughed. "I think I'll pass. You're pretty great at that."

"Something I picked up when I was younger. I like to ride it every now and then for fun. It's not very practical if I'm in a hurry," he smiled. He pointed at the unicycle and the bicycle and asked, "What do you think the difference is between these two?"

"Besides the obvious – the wheels, I mean?" I thought for a second. "The bicycle is probably faster and more practical in the long run. It has more parts and can be more complicated. The unicycle looks just plain tricky and cool!"

Bill laughed and then became sober. "I wanted to show you this, because it's the foundation of something I call 'Tandem Leadership.' It's how the entrepreneur and his #2 work together. On the uni, it's really a solitary adventure – like a solo entrepreneur, a demonstration of skill and balance – you can't but help look at someone riding a unicycle. It's *Uni*que!"

He cracked up at his own joke. "If you compare the unicycle and the bicycle, the unicycle says 'look at me' while the bicycle says 'join me.' How old were you when you had your first bicycle: six, seven, eight? What was the first thing you did?"

"Go find my buddies and go riding." I remembered all the places my two best friends and I would go. Further and further away from our neighborhood, we would ride as we grew and became bolder, and our world became larger. "It's where our adventures began – going fishing or up to the corner gas station when we wanted candy."

"The bicycle needs two wheels – regardless of the number of seats on it. But each wheel has its own purpose. The back wheel is rigid and provides stability, as it's attached to the chain or derailleur, the heart of the transmission for our geared bicycles. Meanwhile, the front wheel can turn as it needs, and direct the bike in any direction. Regardless, both wheels are connected and work together to provide motion for the bike and its rider."

"Tandem Leadership is the joint but separate roles a CEO and his #2 have to hold their business together," he continued, "If the CEO rides around on a unicycle, showing off his talents without any regard to bringing his company and his people along with him, it's not worth much. And two guys riding separate unicycles won't do much for you, either. But if he can find the right person to be his back wheel, to keep the gears moving to support the direction of the CEO and its company, how much more powerful is that? How much further can his company go?"

I thought about the past month. I felt like my life was like the motion of the unicycle: fits and starts and small circles, worrying about falling at any moment. I liked the idea of having someone who could keep the operation running smoothly, and support the company in the direction I thought we should be going. I also understood the value of having two wheels in concert, moving in the same direction at a greater speed than either of them could do on their own. The value of having all the moving parts of my company running together or "in tandem" seemed incredibly appealing to me right now.

"For you and your #2 to work," Bill warned, "you have to know he can lead and support others as well as follow your lead when you're moving the company forward. The bike can only go in one direction. So, can you see Gary as the #2 in your tandem?"

"Yes, I can," I answered, "but by thinking about it like this now, I do have different questions to ask him. I know what I *want* to do, and *have* to do, to move Shelfwerx to the next level. I need to make sure he's able and willing to do the other things I *can't* do to make that happen. That's what you meant the other day, by "hiring the right person for the wrong job," isn't it? It wasn't that Gary wasn't a good prospect for hire, it's just we might not have needed him for the job we have."

"Yes, you're right on there. That's why I wanted you to have a very clear vision on the job you and Shelfwerx need so there will be no mistake what you're asking him to do – both now and as the company grows," Bill said. "Shelfwerx has a very exciting future ahead, Marcus. It's not hard for most people to see what you have here – but whomever you hire needs to be more than just an enthusiastic cheerleader or someone who likes to play street ball or put out fires. They need to make real contributions in helping you run this company."

"I can see that now. It sure gives a different perspective on the term, 'well-oiled machine,'" I laughed. "What do we do now?"

"Let's go back inside and start working on defining the job and take a look at what questions you need to have answered to know if your candidate is a good fit for the job," he said as we walked back to my office. "By the time we're done meeting with Gary, he'll know and you'll know if Shelfwerx is his next stop."

We spent another hour reviewing the top needs emerging from our previous list before Bill left. I still had some work to do to prepare for Gary's interview, but I was excited to see if he would be a good fit to be the Shelfwerx "back tire."

- What are your key tasks and which are the most important to the long term success of your business?
- How do you and your # 2 or second-in-command work together?
- Do you have clearly defined roles for each of your key players?

CHAPTER 5

I went home that night, excited to talk to Maggie about the future of Shelfwerx, encouraged about the possibilities, and buoyed by my conversation with Bill. After the kids were in bed, we went out to the patio to have some rare "grown up" conversation. I know I had been preoccupied with Shelfwerx the past few months. Because it was my passion, and she had understood my vision, Maggie was supportive of my creating Shelfwerx. But she had also always made it clear it was her intention to continue her work as a school therapist when the kids were old enough. In that regard, she expected me to pull my share of the parenting duties – especially as the kids became older, and I could support their activities.

"So," she started, "I received an email today from the district...."

"And?" I waited for the other shoe to drop. Maggie was one of the most direct women I knew, and her demeanor suggested she was going to tell me something I wasn't expecting.

She sighed. "They asked if I would consider coming on staff *four* days a week in January. Alice Peterson just turned in her notice to retire in December. With the hiring freeze, they won't be able to replace her position, *but* they can give me a temporary increase in the number of days I work until next summer, when they can post the position for hire. Because of the way my contract is worded, and my credentialing, I'm the only person in the district they can do this with."

"And you want to say 'yes.'"

"Yes, I think I do."

I thought a moment. I could tell she was torn about going back to work before Cassie was in kindergarten, but was feeling a professional obligation to the teachers and students she worked with. Perhaps because she was the youngest – or it was just her personality – of all our three children, Cassie was the most precocious and self-assured. She would turn four shortly, and be in kindergarten by next year. Even this year, when Cole and Daisy went back to school, Cassie would drag her backpack to the front door and cry as they got on the bus. Maggie found herself giving Cassie "homework" to do in the evenings as Cole and Daisy worked on theirs. She was definitely ready for more, and I told Maggie as much.

"I agree, she is," she said. "But it's more than that. We made this commitment as a family. You know how I feel about commitments – it's important to honor them. And, I'm concerned the business is going to take more of your time, and I'm going to need more of your help to do this."

I could understand what she meant, but I knew we could make it work. Originally, when we had the conversation about starting Shelfwerx, she reminded me she was intent on going back to work full-time when Cassie went to school. I made her a promise I would support her in doing so. At the time, I had a timeframe of over two years to make it work. Now, I had lost one of those years. "Lots of couples both work and raise their kids, Maggie. I know we will be fine, and we can get some help, too."

"I'm not worried about getting help," she said, "I don't care who cleans our house or mows the lawn. Remember when Cole and Daisy were younger, and it was always so frantic because we had to watch them *all the time?*"

I nodded as she went on, "Then one day, Cole got up and made 'breakfast' for both of them while we were still sleeping?"

I did remember. Cole and Daisy were sharing a room then, and Cole taught Daisy how to flip over her crib rail onto his bed so they could both get up before us. We both woke up and there was an immediate panic because we couldn't hear them on the baby monitor. We walked into the kitchen and saw that Cole had pulled a chair to the cupboard and the refrigerator to grab the cereal and milk. They were both happily eating away, chatting as if they had done it for years.

"Well, the thing you don't realize," Maggie said quietly, "is that while we don't need to worry about any of the kids putting their fingers into a light socket or running into the street any more, they know if we are paying attention to them. They know if you don't have time for them. You work more hours now than you did at Diamond Bros., and you're not fully present when you're home. I can tell, you're kind of half in and half out most of the time. And we all notice, Marcus."

We were both quiet in our thoughts for a few minutes before Maggie broke the silence. "The other thing you said when we agreed to start Shelfwerx, was not only did you want to provide for your family, you wanted us to have a better quality of life as a family. I love having nicer things and being able to take trips with the kids, Marcus, and not having to worry about paying our bills. But I would give everything up in a heartbeat if I thought it would give us our best family. You know my dad travelled all the time, and he was never home. I'm not willing to repeat my Mom's life."

Maggie was the more pragmatic one of the two of us, and smarter, as well. I had liked her from the time we first met, though it hadn't dawned on me to ask her out because I didn't think she would say 'yes.' So we hung out in the same group of friends and dated other people for a time, until the fateful weekend of Kyle and Mandy's wedding. During the reception, we had walked out to work on decorating Kyle's car, when she got a phone call from her mother. Her father had just had a heart attack, and was on his way to the hospital. Something in me kicked in, and I offered to drive her to meet them. We spent the next 12 hours waiting with her mom and younger brother until her father was out of surgery and stable. By the time we had finished our tenth cup of coffee, Maggie in her bright pink bridesmaid dress and me in my black tux and pink tie, I had fallen hard. I knew I would do anything to protect her from all the sadness and heartache she had experienced that night. It took me a little longer to convince her, but almost none of our friends were surprised. "About time, Kinsey," was a familiar refrain. I hadn't thought about that time in our lives in a long time, and I realized so much had happened to get us where we were today.

"I can do better, Maggie," I said – and I meant it.

"I know, Marcus," Maggie answered wisely. "But don't do it for me or the kids. Do it for *yourself*. The guy I married was pretty amazing and had great plans to be an even more amazing father. I'd hate for you to miss out on that."

On Thursday morning, I worked with Neil and his guys to set up the Quick Drugstores shelves in the shop. Even with all their modifications, we were going to make the deadline. We still hadn't determined how we were going to package for ease of installation at the customer's facility. But this first install was a test. We'd know more after Neil and I went over there next week to do the install at Quick Drugstores' demo store. I could tell the operators were proud of what they had done, and were excited to see the finished product. I soon found myself talking to Neil about the next anticipated order and delivery, and how we could increase production within our current layout. He and I both could see the opportunity before us, and were looking forward to the challenge. But before I went back to my office, I called Kathy out into the shop, grabbed everyone a soda, and made a toast: "To our first new customer product as Shelfwerx! Thanks for all of your hard work, and I appreciate your flexibility with all the design changes! Cheers!"

I didn't notice Bill had arrived a few minutes earlier. Gary was coming in and Bill had agreed to help interview. He smiled as he walked up, "Looks like a lot of progress since I was here last."

"It sure feels like it," I answered. "Gary should be here soon. Should we go back to my office and finalize our strategy?"

Bill had given me some suggestions on how to frame the interview, based on the discovery process of what I should be doing for the business, and where we needed more help. We were a small company, and being transparent was important to me. Bill had also pointed out that Neil and Kathy would be working with our new hire as much or more than I would be. So including them in the interview process was important. Earlier in the week, I sat down with Kathy and Neil to review the interview process with them. I had expected them to be upset or concerned about bringing in a new person, but both were enthusiastic. Their comments kept coming back to the attraction of having "someone who has time" for them, and "getting stuff done around here." I had to admit, a part of me was a little offended and irritated at them. I told Bill as much, venting a little, as we prepped for Gary to arrive.

"Let me get this straight," he asked, "You have two key employees who are completely dedicated to your endeavor, and they are being completely honest with you. Whose problem is that?"

I stared at him, slightly uncomfortable. He had completely nailed me. "Mine, I guess."

"Marcus," he smiled but then became serious, "If you want to add someone to your team at the level you need, there isn't any room for playing that kind of game. If you're not strong enough to handle another high-level person to truly support you and your company, you're not ready to take the next step. Do you understand what I mean?"

"I think so," I answered. "I've been 'the guy' for a while, and even though it's obvious I need help, I need to be willing to let someone else come be 'the guy' as well. It's that idea of the tandem leaders again – two wheels on the same bike – each with different responsibilities but supporting the movement of the company."

He nodded. "How well Gary or whomever you hire works out will depend as much or more on how well you adjust to the new framework. The most perfect hire will struggle under the weight of your ego or insecurities."

"I get it," I told him. "There's a part of me that wants to be the hero who can save everything around here because it's my company. I know it's unrealistic but...."

"But normal," he finished my sentence and added, "and also dangerous. The longer you play that way, it becomes a harder habit to break – for everyone. It's something we'll need to keep an eye on."

We finished going over the questions and format I had set up. Neil and Kathy would interview Gary first, and then Bill. After they were done, I would show him around the company and he and I would finish the interview. In total, we were planning almost four hours of interviewing. We also reviewed the questionnaire Bill recommended. It was a lengthy version of questions related to the candidate's life, and how they saw their accomplishments and challenges. "It's easier to look for the pebbles that will cause problems before you hire." he said. "Undiscovered, those pebbles can become boulders after new hires come on board."

Gary showed up exactly five minutes early. At Diamond Bros, he always wore one of the signature Diamond Bros golf shirts. Not overly dressed in a full suit and tie, today he was wearing slacks and nice sports jacket. He looked professional, but not unapproachable. I felt myself relax as I realized he was taking this as a serious interview, even though we had known each other for years.

We had organized our small conference room for the interviews, and I found myself getting more curious as the interviews with Kathy and Neil went on for over an hour. It took all my restraint to not pounce on Kathy and Neil to ask for their immediate opinions on Gary. While Bill met with Gary, I decided it was best to keep busy. I immersed myself in the long overdue project of reviewing the new vendor agreements Quick Drugstores had sent over. About 90 minutes later, they were both standing in my doorway.

"I think Gary could use a chance to stretch his legs," Bill said.

"It was a pleasure to meet with you, Gary. I really enjoyed our conversation." Bill shook Gary's hand and looked at me, "Marcus, I'll see you tomorrow around 12?"

"Thanks, Bill," After he left, I looked at Gary and grinned, "Want the fifty-cent tour of the palace?"

Gary and I walked through the plant. I explained what we were doing and what I hoped we could do. He listened well and asked good questions; it seemed as if he was genuinely curious and trying to temper his enthusiasm. We arrived in the area where the Quick Drugstores project was set up. I explained where we were with the project and what our challenges were with the packaging and installation.

"Henry Ford it," he said. I looked at him, clearly not understanding. "Do you know how Henry Ford got his idea for his assembly lines?"

I shook my head. He went on: "It's a way of using deconstruction to think differently. He was inspired by the way the Chicago meat-packing houses worked at the time. In meat packing, they used to 'disassemble' the carcasses and he thought, 'Why can't you do the same for putting something together?' You have the demo shelves all put together – in taking it apart, think about how it needs to be put together and then package it that way. The setup could be put on video and uploaded to a website only your customers could use. Win-win – customers get their setup correct, and the number of service calls you make are reduced."

"Wow … great idea. I'm sure the customers would love it, because they wouldn't need to send a team of facilities folks in each time they changed out to the new shelving solutions. It could be customized to each customer; a lot of their stores have the same base layout," I looked at Gary. "I would have never have thought of it that way. I can't wait to work on this with Neil tomorrow."

I finished the interview in my office, and there I learned more about Gary than I knew before. He and I were around the same age, and he had started working for Diamond Bros a few years before me. Unlike me, he had gotten married and enlisted in the Marines when he was 18. After he was discharged, he went back to college to get his degree while working full-time. He started at Diamond Bros as a night shift supervisor in the Distribution center. He had twin sons in high school, and his wife was a surgical nurse at the local hospital.

I told Gary I would be reviewing the information with the team and getting back to him no later than the following Monday. As he was leaving, he thanked me and said, "Hey, I almost forgot. Bill told me to ask you something."

"What?"

"He wanted me to let you know I'm training for a charity bicycle ride this weekend and thought you might want to go for a ride," he said, looking at me. "I didn't know you cycled."

I just started laughing, "I don't much now, but I have a feeling there's a lot more riding in my future!"

* * *

- What personal sacrifices have you made for your business? Are there any regrets?
- As the "front wheel," what kind of "back wheel" will you need to be paired with to be successful?
- Do you have a strong employee selection process that supports the vision and culture of your company?

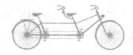

CHAPTER 6

The next morning, Kathy and Neil were waiting for me to discuss Gary.

"How soon can he start?" Neil asked.

"So he did a good job, huh?" I laughed. Thinking about what Bill and I had discussed earlier, I became a little more somber. "This is probably the most important hire of our young company, so I really want to make sure we do a good job in evaluating Gary and how he'll do here. We don't have another candidate to compare him to – yet. But if we're not 100% sure, I will start looking at other people. So, let's review the interview questions and Gary's answers."

Neil and Kathy then proceeded to go through the interview and everything they liked about Gary. They had picked up on some good things he could add to Shelfwerx, and moreover, these were areas where they both needed additional support. When pressed about any concerns they had, they both became quiet and shifted in their chairs. After looking at each other, Kathy spoke up, "Are you sure the *two of you* can work together?"

I started to say I had known Gary for years and we had worked well together at Diamond Bros, but instead asked, "What do you mean?"

Kathy drew a deep breath, "Gary seemed like he likes to *get stuff done* – you like to *think about* things. And well, I just think that difference might cause some problems."

I thought a minute. In my previous work life, no one had ever told me I procrastinated. In fact, just the opposite: I had had a tendency to react too quickly. So I found her comment interesting. Was it the change of becoming the owner of the company? As I had learned over the past few weeks, there were more things to do than I had time for – or at least I thought that was the case.

"Well, that's an interesting observation," I said. "I didn't realize I was doing that. Can you give me an example?"

Kathy then proceeded to give me a list of tasks she felt I had procrastinated on. What I realized is the list of items seemingly important to her was not what I thought important and I had prioritized them accordingly. Kathy thought I was procrastinating, and I thought I was doing a better job in prioritizing my time.

"I can see how you thought that, Kathy," I told them. "But I was just trying to make sure the things I was working on were the most important. That's one of the reasons I want to bring someone like Gary on the team. He was my "go to" guy at Diamond Bros – always willing to find a way to get stuff done for my customers. I think we need that kind of person here now. Thanks for taking the time to interview him and your feedback. I'm going to get Bill's feedback and we'll go from there. I'll keep you posted."

After Neil went back to the shop, I stopped by Kathy's desk. "I appreciate you felt comfortable enough to be honest about how you're feeling working with me."

"Marcus," she laughed. "I worked with your uncle for 15 years, and before that I was the only woman working for the superintendent on a construction site. I know no other way to be!"

"Well, I appreciate it."

Bill and I met for lunch over at Jerry's Top Town Diner for lunch. I realized he was as well-known there as Jake, and I was surprised I had never run into him before. I told him about Neil and Kathy's report out on their interview with Gary, including Kathy's comment about my "procrastination." I went through my interview with Gary, and included his idea about creating setup videos for installations.

"If anything, I like him more for the position than I did before we did the interviews," I told him, "But I'm curious about what you thought of him."

"I liked him and I thought he matches what you told me about him," Bill said, "I think Kathy's comment is interesting, and we should see if there are any other reservations we need to uncover. Let's take a look at the position requirements we developed last week, and see if we can find any problems."

We went through the position requirements item by item – noting anything that might be a concern. When we were done, the list had a just a few items. Bill asked me, "Look at this list, are there any deal breakers on there?"

I reviewed the list and it had three items on it.

- Diamond Bros has more infrastructure than Shelfwerx. Will this be a problem?
- Can I share responsibilities with another person?
- Can we afford to pay him the salary he's making at Diamond Bros?

I was comfortable item #1 would not be an issue for Gary. The new management at Diamond Bros was a lot more formal than most of my career at Diamond Bros. In working with Gary, I knew he thrived as I did before the new management took over the company. In fact, I had made a point of implementing some of the things I liked from my early career at Diamond Bros at Shelfwerx, trying to replicate their culture.

"I know Kathy and Neil are concerned I don't want to share responsibilities with another person – probably because I haven't delegated to them as much as they want," I told Bill, "but I think I know now this company is stuck with me doing everything by myself so I have to change. I want to change."

"I know we can't offer Gary the kind of package he has at Diamond Bros. Do you have any thoughts on how to make it work?" I asked Bill.

"I do," he said. He looked in his notebook "Do you remember what the three items were on your list we hashed out a few weeks ago? I have them here – getting new sales/ closing deals, new product ideas, and cash management. What's it worth to you to increase your focus on these activities – spend 50% more of your time than you are now?"

"Well," I pondered. "If I wasn't dealing with all the other stuff, I could probably close three to five more deals like Quick Drugstores and Penny's Pantry pretty quickly. Our sales could be at least double what we've forecasted for this next year. So, I can put real numbers on it."

"There's the strategy piece. Now, you have to make the cash part of it work." Bill said. "If you can do that, I think you have a candidate."

I left lunch knowing what I needed to do. I went back to the office and ran the various scenarios of adding more customers at a quicker pace than I originally anticipated. I also did some "worst case" scenarios, to see what it would do to our cash position if we couldn't convert as quickly as I had thought. I sent our CPA an email with some updated budgeting information for his review. After being comfortable I had covered everything, I sent out an email update to Jake. I didn't need his permission to hire Gary, but I also had made a promise to keep him abreast of what was going on at Shelfwerx, and I wasn't going to let him think I had forgotten. Besides, if he had any objections, I wanted to know sooner than later. In looking at the case I had made for offering Gary a position at Shelfwerx, I felt pretty confident he would know we were making the right decision.

On Sunday morning, I received an email from Jake.

Marcus:

Thanks for the update. Sounds like you and Bill have thought everything through and things are going well. We are having a great trip! Molly sends her love to you and Maggie and the kids.

Jake

I knew Gary went to work early, so I called him on my way into the office. I offered him the position, and asked if he had any questions or concerns. While the salary offer was close to what he was currently making at Diamond Bros, our CPA at Hunter Jackson, Bill, and I thought we could create an even bigger incentive for making the sales and delivery targets we would be able to do with Gary on our team.

"Marcus, actually, I don't have any questions. Since Diamond Bros was sold, I've been preparing myself for a job change. I never would have interviewed if I wasn't ready to say yes to the right opportunity. You did an awesome job in presenting the opportunities and challenges, and I'm ready to come on board," Gary said. I could tell he was smiling through the phone. I had worked on his offer letter over the weekend, and told him I would email it to him shortly. He said he would give notice that day, and I'd see him in two weeks.

When I arrived at the office, I found a note from Neil saying they were readying to work on the packaging of the Quick Drugstores delivery. After Gary's interview, I had told Neil about Gary's idea about "Henry Fording it." We had hashed around some ideas on Friday afternoon and Neil and his guys had come up with a great plan. As it turned out the son of one of the machine operators was going to college in television production, and he did wedding videos on the side. While he had originally volunteered his time if he could use the video for his portfolio, I had decided to pay him instead, as some of what we filmed might be considered proprietary – either by Quick Drugstores or Shelfwerx. I told him if he did a good job, there'd be more opportunities and he was thrilled.

So I was more than thrilled when I got out to the shop and saw how organized everything was. Neil had the most experience with our installs, but didn't want to be on camera. Lenny, a younger guy who loved to talk, had volunteered. They had conducted one run-through and were excited to show me the video. Even unedited, I could see the value and knew how I could use it with Quick Drugstores to strengthen the sale. I gave them some minor feedback, and they wanted to try again. By the end of the day, they had actually done the on-camera run through the setup and take down three times.

Neil stopped by my office before he left for the day.

"The guys seemed to have some fun today," he told me. "But I never thought they would have taken it so seriously. We ended up with a little bonus, too."

"What do you mean?" I asked, "Lenny's going to start doing stand-up comedy?"

He laughed, "What a goofball that guy is, but I have to admit he really got into it and did a good job."

He proceeded to tell me when the guys had looked at the video and saw how the customer would have to do the installation; they came up with a new way to label the parts. "We won't have it ready for the installation at Quick Drugstores, but I'd like to show it to you tomorrow and see if we want to incorporate it into our next design phase. I think it will save us some money, and make the installs a lot easier for everybody."

After Neil left, I closed my door and took a few minutes to reflect. Everything was going to be different. What did that mean? I looked through all the work Bill and I had done over the past month. My plan was in front of me; now it was time to focus on *the front wheel*.

- Who in your life gives you honest feedback?
- How well do you communicate the vision and needs of the company to your team?
- What is your "go to" strategy for dealing with problems? How does that serve you and your business?

CHAPTER 7

Tuesday morning was the install at Quick Drugstores. Neil and the guys loaded up the delivery truck, and I was going to meet Neil and Lenny over at Quick Drugstores at 9:00 a.m. We were fortunate to be so close to their headquarters, and they had been adding quite a few new stores over the past two years. I was hoping this was the beginning of a long, prosperous relationship – and that our product could become their standard.

Since this was the Quick Drugstores concept store, the team we would work with was accustomed to having different vendors in and out of their store along with the headquarters brass, Vaughn Tappan explained to me. He had given us the name of the store manager, as well as his project manager, so I was surprised when Vaughn met us at the store.

I introduced Neil and Lenny to Vaughn and his team. While they were unloading, Vaughn and I surveyed the area where the installation was going to take place. We discussed how their installations typically worked, and what problems they encountered. Within his division, he supervised a number of teams that renovated and updated merchandising fixtures and layouts as well as trained store staff on how to perform minor changes to layouts and installations, depending on the season or assortments. I told him about our plans to include demo videos to simplify installations and adjustments to layouts. He seemed genuinely pleased at the idea. Gary had already won one for us, and he hadn't even started working at Shelfwerx yet.

It was early afternoon by the time we got back to the shop. I had sent both Bill and Jake an email about Gary's acceptance of the position. Bill had emailed a lengthy response, so I poured myself a cup of coffee and sat down to read it.

Marcus:

Good to hear about Gary. As you know I will be out of town for the next two weeks, and I wanted to leave you a few things to start "test riding" your new leadership structure at Shelfwerx.

1. *Starting tomorrow, I'd like you to begin your day as if Gary was already on board and at Shelfwerx. Look at your "To Do" List – determine what he would be doing that day, think about each*

interaction you have with Kathy or Neil, and decide who would be responsible for making that decision: you or Gary. Write at least 5 things down Gary would be doing each day.

2. *Look at your personal "to do" list. Pick something to start now. If you can't think of anything, I'm sure Maggie will have a suggestion or two!*

3. *Develop a 90-day project list for Gary. Once he arrives, the pace is going to pick up and you need to be prepared. This may surprise you, but most new employees are under-challenged in their first few weeks because their supervisor doesn't want to overwhelm them. High performers would prefer to be contributing as soon as possible.*

Think of it like this. Everything should be different — but if you don't start mentally preparing for the difference, everything will stay the same. This is the practice or the preparation for the race. It's the beginning of adding the back wheel to your bicycle.

Drop me a note at the beginning of next week to check in and let me know if you have any questions.

Regards,

Bill

P.S. Bicycles don't travel backwards — they need to be turned around.

I closed the email. "Bicycles don't travel backwards"? What did that mean? I had thought I'd get a break while

Bill was on vacation, and some time to reflect before Gary started. I had to start acting as if Gary was already here? How was I supposed to do that? After a good morning at Quick Drugstores, I was tired and frustrated. I told Kathy I had an appointment out of the office, and wouldn't be coming back for the remainder of the day. She took one look at me and knew not to ask any questions.

I got in my car. Then, I realized that while I didn't want to be at the office, I didn't exactly have a destination in mind. I found myself taking the back roads out of town up to the old River Road. When I had worked at Diamond Bros, I had spent a lot of time driving – either visiting my customers or traveling with my sales guys to visit their customers. Shelfwerx was just a few miles from our house. While a short commute had its advantages, I noticed I had missed the time alone in the car. To be more productive, I would make calls as I was driving, but often I just liked being by myself and playing my own music. Removing that time from my daily routine, and reducing my time at the gym, gave me very little time on my own in the last year.

As I left town, I turned onto the River Road. I decided to follow it up to the dam, cross the river and come back down the other side. When I got up to the dam, I stopped at the lookout and got out of the car. It was a beautiful spring day, and I could see for miles. The dam had been built before I was born. I had only known it as one side of the lake where we went fishing and picnicking as kids, and where Maggie and I took our kids now. There was a display of the history of the dam construction. It also included pictures of the flooding that routinely had occurred in our city – as well as other towns along the river before the dam was built – and how the new flow of water downstream allowed for different wildlife habitats, along with people using the new lake for boating and fishing.

I imagined what it had been like before the dam. A lazy river swelling beyond its banks every spring until someone decided there needed to be a different course. There would be sacrifices – the lake the dam created consumed acres of land – but there would be benefits, too. Towns wouldn't flood, and a new lake would create a park, new habitat, other forms of commerce. It was completely different now – in fact, the very spot where I was now standing didn't even exist (as land) then. Just like two years ago, Shelfwerx didn't exist, and now it did. I had wanted to start Shelfwerx – actually, I *had to* start Shelfwerx, there really wasn't a choice in my mind. And now I was frustrated because there was *one more* thing I needed to do? There would *always be* one more thing to do. I couldn't go backwards unless I decided to turn myself around. Changing course was a conscious decision, just as Bill had written in his email.

By mid-afternoon, I was back at home alone. Maggie and the kids were going to visit her cousin out at their farm. I grabbed my gym bag from the far reaches of my closet, and headed to the gym. It had been more weeks than I could remember since I had been there. There was a "pardon our dust" sign at the sign-in desk, and I asked the clerk what they were doing.

"We just upgraded all the cardio and they are moving everything around. Some of the machines won't be available until tomorrow," she told me. Sure enough, I went over to the cardio machine area of the gym and couldn't believe it. Only the stationary bikes were set up and available.

I just started laughing. *I get it, Bill. I get it.*

I spent a full two hours working out at the gym. While my body ached because of it, I went into the office the next day with renewed enthusiasm. Somehow, Bill's email seemed less daunting, and after reviewing it again, I understood where he was pointing me. I had been operating solo, for the most part, since I started Shelfwerx. There were other employees, and Jake, and then of course Bill, all assisting me. But now, my business was on the verge of great possibilities. I needed to raise myself to work in a way that was going to allow another talented, high achieving individual to be successful. And we had to work together – in tandem – if *the company* was to be successful.

At first, following Bill's instructions, I felt unable to make any decision. I found myself questioning everything I was doing, and taking endless notes. By the end of the week, I noticed there were some clear trends. Some operational items were making me crazy. No matter how often Kathy, Neil, or I seemed to discuss what to do, their tasks just kept coming back into our discussions. Clearly, we were not getting to a resolution, and it seemed to be taking up an enormous amount of energy on all of our parts. Additionally, those interruptions or problems were keeping me from doing some of the more strategic items Bill and I had identified as items that *only* I could do. I easily saw how our sales growth was being impacted by my inability to get out of the day-to-day management of the business.

Maggie was thrilled when I shared Bill's email, as she had been bugging me to get back into the gym. I had always been athletic, and she had noticed early on in our relationship how irritable I became when I wasn't physically active. We also agreed to have a night out without the kids – either with friends, or by ourselves. It wasn't only my work schedule that had curtailed our social lives. The kids' activities and schedules had made it just as challenging. However, the new business was the most often used excuse. I was no longer going to allow it to be the reason we put our life on hold.

By the time Gary came on board, I had developed a very aggressive plan for our first 90 days, and I was eager to share it with him. His first weeks at Shelfwerx would be busy. Vaughn Tappan from Quick Drugstores had contacted me, and wanted to discuss next steps. We had set up a meeting at the end of Gary's first week. Gary was familiar with Penny's Pantry, as they also had been a Diamond Bros customer, so learning about the Quick Drugstores business was a must. For the first time, I realized I had another person actually working in the company who could help support the forward momentum of the business. And it felt good.

- Do you have 90-day plans? Why or why not?
- Do you plan into your week adequate time to renew yourself, both physically and mentally?
- How closely do your actions match your intent?

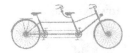

CHAPTER 8

Kathy had taken it upon herself to organize Gary's office. It was small, but I knew Gary wouldn't care. He was accustomed to being in the warehouse, so it was to no surprise that not long after he arrived on Monday, he and I were walking through the building again reviewing our plans. I observed him as he interacted with the guys in the shop. He asked good questions and he listened to their answers. He took notes.

Kathy popped her head out into the plant, "Marcus, James from Hunter Jackson is on the phone. Do you want to take his call?"

I needed to take his call, and Gary motioned at me to go ahead as he and Neil were deep in conversation. I spent the next few hours responding to calls, and after lunch, Gary and I reviewed the 90-day plan and the tasks I wanted to move over to him. He didn't balk or say it was too aggressive. Bill was right. Gary was a high performer and he was up for the challenge. I let him know about the Quick Drugstores meeting at the end of the week.

"Marcus, if you're okay with it, I'd like to spend my time with Neil and Kathy this week," he said. "Once I get to know what they're doing, I think I'll be able to put some more specific timelines on the 90-day plan. That will keep me plenty busy this week while you are prepping for the Quick Drugstores meeting."

The strategy made sense to me. "Sounds great! That's what you're here for and it's all yours."

We both kept focused on our tasks throughout the week. I had briefed Kathy and Neil on the plan for Gary to work with them more closely, and they were enthusiastic. My preparation for the Quick Drugstores meeting was going well. Penny's Pantry had been a long time client of Diamond Bros, and I knew their operation well. With Quick Drugstores, I had done some quick research after our initial meetings, but now I needed to go deeper if we were going to have a good meeting with them at the end of the week. Vaughn Tappan had mentioned they had a growth strategy, but it was much more aggressive than I had thought. Their CEO, Jerry Quick, had been quoted about having a multi-state presence within the next two years. More stores, more renovations all meant great things for Shelfwerx – if we could become their vendor of choice.

I was so engrossed in the work I was doing; I didn't notice the changes at first. But by Thursday, it was obvious to me I was no longer Neil and Kathy's "go to" person for answering questions and problem solving. Gary and I had agreed to check in on Thursday afternoon, and I was looking forward to an update as well as sharing my plans for the Quick Drugstores meeting.

"So, what do you think?" I asked.

"Well, it's been a great week so far. You have a great team here...." he started.

I interrupted him, "You mean 'we' have a great team, don't you?"

He laughed, "You're right. It will probably take me a while to forget I'm not working at Diamond Bros anymore. Yes, we have a great team here, though I do have some concerns. Do you want to hear them?"

I did and he went on: "Did you know Neil doesn't really use the computer? Kathy has been doing all of his computer work for him. I think it could be a problem for us in the future as we grow."

I was surprised. Not that Kathy was covering for Neil, but that I had missed it. Gary had only been here four days. He must have sensed my surprise because he went on, "Look, Marcus, I've spent my whole career working with line employees. When I started at Diamond Bros, they were in the process of going from a manual system to the management system they still have. It's one of the reasons I moved up so fast; most of the old timers didn't want to have anything to do with learning a computer inventory system. With Neil, I don't think he *can't* use a computer, I just think he's uncomfortable with it for some reason."

"I'm afraid to ask now," I said, "what other things are on your list?"

Gary had a longer list than I had anticipated. Some highlights included some minor safety issues in the plant, Kathy was struggling with the new payroll system I approved, we needed to automate our customer invoicing to real time, the shop wanted to move to a four-day work week, and he suspected the new guy was smoking pot in his car during lunch.

I knew having another set of eyes and another pair of hands would change the dynamics of the company but listening to Gary, I realized I had only thought of it in one way: removing things from my long task list. Obviously, I had missed a few things, and I hadn't thought about the discovery of new problems and how we would address them.

"Sounds like everything isn't all that great, then." I knew I sounded defensive, but I couldn't help myself.

Gary paused, "Right now, this week, will be my only time to see Shelfwerx with fresh eyes. When I said there's a great team here, I meant it. The people, the product, and the potential are all amazing. But it doesn't mean there are things that can't be improved. I guess I thought that's one of the reasons you wanted to have me on board."

"You're right – it is," I sighed, "but if I'm going to be honest, I can't believe I missed so many things. We're not that big of an operation – yet."

"That's why it's so important we fix these things as we go," Gary said. "Marcus, this is your company, so I can understand why you are taking this personally. But I dealt with this stuff all of the time at Diamond Bros. The positive *far outweighs* the negative here. You want to hear the good stuff, too?"

He then proceeded to give me a list of items he was excited about, which included a lot of the things I saw in the company. What I realized in listening to him was that Gary was balanced in how he described both problems and opportunities. He had the same enthusiasm for how dedicated the employees were to Shelfwerx, as the need to fix the safety problems in the shop. He was probably one of the most even, unflappable people I had ever met – and I knew he would be a stabilizing force for Shelfwerx.

"So, it sounds like you have learned a lot in a few days and identified some key issues," I told him and then asked, "What do you think we should do to solve these problems?"

"Before I answer your question, I need to ask you something. How do you want us to work together?" he asked.

"What do you mean?"

"I know we both came out of Diamond Bros, Marcus," Gary said, "and we've worked together for years. We worked together very well, in fact. But, in thinking about it, knowing each other well is almost a problem. I assumed because we both worked together before, we could just start where we left off back at Diamond Bros. But, this is a completely different company. This is *your* company, and I feel like we skipped a step. With everything we've discussed, we haven't talked about how you want us to work together."

I thought of all my discussions with Bill, and realized I had been so consumed at getting Gary in to start working on the list

I had created for him, we had neglected to discuss how we were going to operate as a leadership team. The Shelfwerx "tandem leadership" team.

"So, have you ever heard of 'Tandem Leadership'?" I asked. I then went through all I had learned from Bill over the past few weeks. I drew a rough drawing of a bicycle.

"A wheel by itself, like a unicycle, can operate on its own. It might be interesting to watch, but it can't go very fast and it's not very stable," I started, "but when you add the frame and a second wheel, you've got a machine – not just some entertainment. The back wheel creates stability. It focuses on keeping the machine moving."

"And the front wheel is the vision. It keeps the bike moving in the right direction," Gary said, "which is why it might have been harder for you to see some of things I've noticed this week. If you've been looking forward, especially far down the road, it's harder to see what's around you."

"I hadn't thought about it like that," I said, "but it makes sense. I've been so preoccupied with the future of the company; I haven't wanted to pay attention to the some of the operational stuff. Kathy and Neil are great, but some days, I just wanted them to call in sick so I could get some work done."

Gary laughed, "I understand. I've never heard of Tandem Leadership but I like the idea of it. You know I ride, right? It makes a lot of sense to me. I can see why you like it."

I shared more of what Bill had taught me about Tandem Leadership, and how I was anxious to put it into practice for Shelfwerx. We decided while I had done a good job in putting together Gary's 90-day task list, I had neglected to put one together for me or for the company. Without at least some understanding of what I was trying to do, Gary's ability to make good decisions to support the overall company goals was going to be limited. As Gary said, we had a great bike and knew all the destinations we wanted to see – but no road map for our trip. It was up to us to put the road map in place. Because we were going to be at Quick Drugstores on Friday, and I had to leave early to coach at Cole's baseball practice, we decided to reconvene on Monday to work on our coordinated plan.

The next day, we drove together over to Quick Drugstores headquarters to meet Vaughn Tappan and his team. After introducing everyone, Vaughn said, "Marcus, Gary – we appreciate having you come over here today. The initial feedback from our concept store on your product has been quite good, and even in these first few weeks, we're seeing some increase in performance in the assortments using the Shelfwerx products. We still need more testing and validation before we would consider awarding you an additional contract, but we'd like to have you start preparing a bid for us. As you know, Shelfwerx has a confidentiality agreement with Quick Drugstores, and what I'm about to review with you is part of that confidentiality agreement."

He then started to review their five-year detailed expansion program. It was much more aggressive than the information I had found in my research. They planned to move out into the four neighboring states, and double the number of their stores both by building new stores and by acquisition. In addition, their new branding effort would require all stores to be updated. Depending on how much of their products they wanted to move into Shelfwerx fixtures, it could represent significant revenue over a number of years, giving us some stability while we continued to grow the company. It was hard to pay attention to Vaughn's detailed presentation as I found myself doing all sorts of calculations in my head on the amount of product we'd need to produce, and what that meant for the future of the company.

"The reason I wanted to sit down with you, Marcus, is our proof of concept period on the Shelfwerx products will end on the 15th," he said, pulling out another document. "Our bid packet is going to be due on the 31st. The turnaround is short, mainly because we want to start replacing shelves for the Christmas launch in October in some designated stores on the renovation list. At this count, it is about 50 locations. The number could grow by the time the final decision is made. We're very interested in the Shelfwerx product, and here's a copy of the bid requirements."

"Vaughn, I'm thrilled," I said. Quick Drugstores would be our largest customer by the end of the year.

"Great," he smiled. And then his tone changed. "We do have some concerns, Marcus, which is another reason we wanted to meet with you in person, and why we asked Samantha and Amanda to join us."

Samantha Alsted was the Director of Vendor Management, and Amanda Perry was the concept store manager. Samantha told us Quick Drugstores wanted to consider Shelfwerx products for most of the candy, snack, and small sundry aisles. She then proceeded to let us know that because our company was so new, Shelfwerx was coming up very low on their traditional vendor scoring system. Unfortunately, based on the total dollar volume of the potential purchase and our score, Shelfwerx technically wasn't qualified to bid on the project. Because they considered our products "specialized," they had a waiver in place for us to bid with special requirements.

Before I could ask any questions, Amanda started speaking. She had a list of issues and concerns she and her team had discovered while working with the Shelfwerx products at the demo store. The Quick Drugstores store team thought the shelves did a great job in displaying the product, however, they had found them difficult to change out by themselves when updating the displays. They also thought some of the components weren't uniform, which created problems in moving the displays. She passed over a detailed report to Gary and me with a detailed list they would like to see corrected.

I felt ambushed, but I had been in enough sales negotiations to know it was important to keep a level head. All my interactions with Vaughn had been completely different, but we hadn't been working with him or Quick Drugstores all that long for me to know if this was their standard procedure. Before I could speak, Gary asked Amanda a question. "Amanda, I'm new to Shelfwerx, actually, this is day number five for me, so I'm not as familiar with the Shelfwerx product as everyone here. The report is great, but I'm wondering if it's possible for us to go over to your store so you could show us your concerns? Sometimes, for a shop guy like me it's easier to see things in person."

"I think that's a great idea, Gary," Vaughn said. "Amanda and I will meet you over there and everyone can head out for the day after we're done."

Samantha excused herself. "It was great meeting you both. I'll be your contact for questions on your bid. Let me know if you have any questions."

We got in the car and I turned to Gary, "Thanks for the save, there. What I wanted to say and what I was going to say were pretty different. I haven't worked with them long enough to know all the ins and outs of their organization."

"Well, I couldn't tell either but I thought I could use the 'I'm new' card at least once to get us out of there," he laughed. "It seems to me like Vaughn is trying to be an advocate for Shelfwerx, but I couldn't tell with the other two."

We drove over to the demo store, and Amanda and one of her assistant managers started showing us the problems they were having. It quickly became apparent they were reconfiguring the shelving in a way it wasn't designed to work. Both Gary and I could see what their problem was, and Gary started asking questions to determine what changes they would need to meet their needs.

Vaughn pulled me aside. "I didn't mean to blindside you today. Even with the issues Amanda presented today, a number of us are optimistic about Shelfwerx – which is why we wanted to give you a heads up on what is coming down the pike. By the way, Amanda's full name is Amanda Quick Perry. She's Jerry Quick's daughter. She's been working her way through the business, and now she's on the retail side. She's a good kid, but has a little chip on her shoulder. If you can score a win with her at the store, it will definitely help."

"Thanks, Vaughn, I understand," and I did. Jerry Quick was the son of the founder of Quick Drugstores, and the current Chairman. I looked over at Gary and Amanda. Gary was taking notes and pictures with his phone. They both looked pleased. I couldn't wait to let Gary know he was charming the heir apparent.

- How well do you receive constructive criticism? Do you have someone on your team who can provide you that feedback?
- How often do you incorporate customer feedback into your strategy?
- What does having a strategic partner mean to you?

CHAPTER 9

On the way back from Quick Drugstores, Gary and I were able to start working on a strategy to update the Quick Drugstores fixtures as well as a plan for gaining their future business. When I dropped him off, he asked me if I wanted to meet over at Shelfwerx on Saturday to continue our planning.

I started to say "yes," but it had been a long week with more than enough late nights in our future. I thought about how I wanted my professional and work life to be different now that he was on board. So, instead I told him, "Why don't we take the weekend off? I have a feeling if everything keeps going as we heard today, there will be more than enough opportunities for us to spend our Saturdays at Shelfwerx."

"Well, I just wanted to offer," he said, "I'm excited to get started on retrofitting those fixtures with Neil on Monday. Amanda and her team won't know what hit them when they see the replacement parts."

As Gary left the car I told him, "Thanks for a great week, Gary. I appreciate your candor. We're both strong people, so I know it's probably not the last time we'll have some differences, but I was glad to have you at Quick Drugstores today. By the way, Bill is back from his vacation and will be coming into the office on Monday. I'd like us to meet with him then to learn more about how we can work on our Tandem Leadership skills and get his take on Quick Drugstores."

I slept well on Friday night, and Maggie had planned a full weekend for us. I had been tempted to take Gary up on his offer to work on Saturday. It was refreshing to have someone to talk to and work with at a new level in the company. But I heard both Maggie and Bill in my head, and I knew if I didn't make the commitment to myself and my family to start operating differently on how I was prioritizing my life, the full benefit of having Gary on board wouldn't be realized.

When Cole and I came home after his baseball practice on Saturday, the girls and Maggie were outside. Maggie was working in her flower beds while the girls were playing. Cassie flew up to the car.

"Cassie, whoa! Remember what Daddy and Mommy said about waiting until the car is stopped?" I asked her.

"Daddy, Daddy, Daddy!" She was breathless and then exclaimed, "You have to watch! Mommy and Daisy practiced with me. I can do it all by myself. Sit on the porch with Cole."

"Okay," I told her and smiled at Cole. "Your sister's wish is our command, I guess. Let's go, buddy."

"Wait until you see, Daddy, Cassie is pretty good," Daisy said, seriously.

I waved at Maggie, "I've been summoned to watch Cassie do something."

"Oh, you'll be surprised," she came up to the porch and sat between me and Cole.

I heard the girls in the garage, and Maggie just smiled. Then Daisy, who was nine, came out of the garage, "Ladies and gentlemen. The Amazing Cassandra would like your attention, please."

Out of the garage came Cassie, riding on her sister's hand-me-down starter bicycle, up the walkway to meet us. The training wheels were missing, and Daisy was walking next to the bike. Cassie was beaming from ear to ear. I looked at Maggie then. "Did you take off her training wheels?"

"No, I did not," she answered. She looked at Cole and Daisy. "Apparently, it was a conspiracy that neither of us was aware of."

I looked at Cole and he looked sheepish. "Dad, she was bugging us so much. We just did it to get her to leave us alone. But it didn't work."

"What do you mean 'it didn't work'?"

"Daisy and I took the training wheels off, and then she really started to be mad at us until we said we would help her ride," he looked at Maggie. "We always made sure she had her helmet on."

Maggie was trying hard not to laugh. Cole was so serious, and thought he was in trouble until he saw the corners of his mother's mouth turn up.

"Well, I appreciate you taking the lead, son, but make sure you check in with us before you teach her how to drive a car," I got up and gave Daisy a break as I took over chasing Cassie around the driveway until she was tired of riding.

Monday came quickly. I arrived early, but even then Gary was already out in the shop with Neil. Some of the concerns the Quick Drugstores concept store expressed had been identified in the videos we had done the previous week, so Neil and the guys had already started working on it. Even though I hadn't done any "real" work over the weekend, I thought about Shelfwerx a lot, and how I wanted the company and my life to be different. I was glad Bill was coming in today, and looking forward to hashing out some of my thoughts. I also knew it would be good for Gary to learn more about Tandem Leadership and how the two of us could start using it to work better together.

I gathered all the information Bill and I had put together over the past eight weeks, and brought it into the conference room. I realized how much thinking and strategizing we had done. Even though I knew Gary was sharp, I had to believe pulling this information together into an easy plan was going to help tremendously.

I had a few minutes alone with Bill before Gary joined us. Bill looked tan and rested. I still marveled at how young he looked. I updated him on Quick Drugstores and everything that had happened while he was away. Jake had told me that after coming back to run his parents' company, Bill had owned and sold over five companies in his lifetime. He certainly didn't look any worse for the experience.

"Sounds like Vaughn Tappan is on your side," Bill said. "Someone in his position typically doesn't go out on a limb unless he really sees a benefit. That's good. Have you rerun the numbers yet for sales, capacity, and production to accommodate what they are proposing?"

"Gary and I talked about it on the way home. I'm going to map out a sales and delivery strategy, and he's going to look at the capacity issues with Neil. Then we'll get together and determine next steps," I told him. "This could change everything. When I started the company, I knew what the market potential was with convenience stores, but adding a customer like Quick Drugstores could accelerate growth much faster. It's going to be a fun ride."

"What's going to be a fun ride?" Gary had joined us. He shook hands with Bill and sat down. He grinned, "Tour de France, the Smithville 150?"

"I was just telling Bill about the sales potential at Quick Drugstores. How did it go with Neil?"

Gary updated us on the shop. Bill was nodding his head, and I enjoyed knowing Gary was both learning the ropes and able to jump right in. After he was done, I turned to Bill. "Gary and I want to learn more about Tandem Leadership. I think we both know about the basics, but I see all the notes we've compiled over the past few weeks, and I'm not quite sure how to put it into action."

Bill grinned. "Well, why don't we start now?"

"You both understand the basic concepts," Bill went to the white board and started drawing a simple bicycle. "Each of you knows what your role or your wheel is. Each wheel is independent from the other, but in order to move the bike forward, they need to act in concert. Marcus, you should have already done some work on this if you followed the homework assignment."

I nodded. "We reviewed it last week."

"Great," he went on. "Understanding the role or the function is a key, but where to go?"

Gary and I smiled at each other, and Gary said, "Yeah, we figured out that we had lots of destinations but no plan on when we were trying to get there. And I guess we're not quite sure who controls the brakes?"

"Excellent!" he exclaimed. "We're halfway there. Here are the basics: Roles/Wheels, Plan/Destination, Pace/Gears, and Check-in/Gauges. So, tell me, what happens in the case bicycle brakes, if only one is applied at a time?"

"Well, from personal experience, unfortunately," Gary laughed, "if the front brake is put on solo, the rider has a good chance of flying over the handle bars. It's not as dramatic with the back brake, but it does make the front wheel get a little squirrelly and the bike is more difficult to control."

"Interesting analogy isn't it," Bill went on, "if the front wheel is stopped, alone, without the back brake, you're in danger of crashing. Can you think what that means in real terms for Shelfwerx and the two of you?"

"I see it two different ways," I answered him. "If I stop suddenly, or pivot quickly to take the company in a different direction without respecting the operational part of the company, the bike will crash. And, if operations moves faster than the strategy or vision, the same thing can happen, essentially putting the brakes on the front wheel and knocking the rider off the bike."

"Perfect. Gary – now how about only applying the back wheel brakes?" Bill asked.

"Braking the back wheel creates drag on the bike," he answered, looking at me. "If operations can't keep pace with the strategy/vision piece, then Marcus is going to get frustrated. He's going to feel like he's pulling a load behind him, and the bike is going to get off-balance."

"So, these are just some of the items, I call 'The Rules of the Road – Avoiding Flat Tires.'" Bill went back up to the white board and wrote the following under "Rules of the Road."

1. Know Thy Wheel
2. Choose a Destination
3. Use the Right Gears
4. Brake Together
5. Select the Correct Tread

"What do you mean by 'use the right gears'?" I asked.

"When you are going up a hill, Gary, what happens?" Bill asked.

"It gets harder, so you shift down until you find your gear," he answered.

"Correct!" Bill exclaimed. "As the business goal gets harder to execute, or there are more unknowns, you should consider making smaller steps – or, more minor adjustments. Similarly, when everything is clicking, it's like being on the open road and kicking it into high gear to make as much progress as possible. It's one of the biggest mistakes I see organizational leaders making. They hit a bump in the road, and instead of shifting, they choose a different road or to get off the bike altogether. Know your journey is going to use *all* the gears on your bike. Learning to adjust will get you to your destination in one piece, and it will probably be more enjoyable."

I could see what he was saying. Over the past few months, I had been determined to keep moving, but I easily saw how the "bumps" I had encountered could have thrown me and Shelfwerx off track. "Select the tread? Do you mean pick the right tire for the road? The tread is...."

"Resources: people, equipment, support," Bill answered. "Mountain bike tires won't let you be as fast on the road, and vice versa. Evaluate your road conditions, and know what you need. That, too, is a dynamic process."

"It seems like everything is a dynamic process," Gary mused. "How do we keep everything on track?"

"Keeping an eye on the gauges, the check-in process," Bill answered. "It should be as simple as possible, but comprehensive enough to keep the bike going. A child's starter bike is much different than a professional cyclist would ride in the Tour de France. Yet, they both do the same thing. Shelfwerx just took its training wheels off, but I'd expect it to need a much better, bigger bike in the next few months."

I thought about watching Cassie ride without her training wheels. She had fallen a few times, but it never occurred to her to not get on the bike again. She would ride that bike until she outgrew it, and then we'd think nothing of replacing it with another bike when she was ready. Thinking of Shelfwerx in the same way made it easier for me to think about growing the company and dealing with the changes that were sure to come. It was important to train for the big race, but also adjust for the bumps and detours as well.

Over the next few weeks, Bill worked with us to develop our roadmap and our check-in tools, and refine our skills in managing our wheels. Gary and I had made the decision that whenever we hit a problem or a bump in a road, we'd put it on list to hash out during our daily 15-minute "water break" or our weekly one-hour "race planning" meeting. At first, I found some of the analogies and metaphors Bill used a little silly. But as Gary and I started using them more, and teaching the concepts to the rest of the Shelfwerx team, I realized the huge payoff in leveraging the common language and understanding of what we were trying to accomplish. It gave everyone confidence about troubleshooting and addressing any issues that came up. I could see a Shelfwerx bicycle rally in our future.

As promised, we addressed the fixture problems with the Quick Drugstores concept store. Amanda Perry endorsed our status as an approved vendor, and we submitted our bid to provide the required shelving and fixtures for their proposed renovations. It was not a given that we would receive the bid, but the follow up questions coming from their purchasing department were encouraging. Gary and I had been able to attend another trade show and had gotten a great deal of interest from some regional grocery stores, which had been a surprise. A few were working on a "store within a store" concept, and had some different needs than their current vendors were providing them. We had provided three new proposals and some sample fixtures for them to demo.

Jake and Molly had arrived home a few days earlier. He and Molly wanted to unpack and take care of any housekeeping issues, but we were planning on meeting tomorrow. He had left me a voicemail message on my phone: "Can't wait to hear about Shelfwerx, Marcus. See you at the game!"

Cole's baseball team had done well this season, and we were hosting the league championship that night. I thought back to the beginning of the season. I had doubted I would have even had the time to go to his games, let alone help coach the team, if I had not made some changes with Jake's urging and Bill's help. Maggie was right, I would have regretted missing this experience.

Shortly before 3:00 p.m., I started packing up my things for the ride home (yes, I was biking back and forth to work each day by this time) when I heard the familiar ping of my email notification. It was from Vaughn Tappan. I did a quick glance, and smiled. I was thrilled, and Gary and Jake and the rest of the Shelfwerx team would be as well. Off to the ballpark.

I couldn't wait to tell Bill.

- How do you accommodate "bumps" in the road?
- What would you do if you had no limitations in your business?
- Are you ready for your next big opportunity?

CONCLUSION

There is a natural tension in entrepreneurial companies – especially in the beginning – with the push and pull between the desire to grow, and the need to stretch resources. Perhaps you find yourself more extended than you had imagined, both personally and professionally. Maybe in your former job or profession you were exceptional, or a shining star. But you never truly felt the passion for your work until you started your own endeavor. Yet the challenge of balancing everything – in other words, the tasks you are good at and those which you like to do, with the ones that are new and you feel unsure of – becomes stressful. It takes you away from the very thing that motivated you to start the business in the first place: the desire to be independent, and to create and deliver a product you are passionate about.

It is not a coincidence that the skills and talents in which we excel may also create problems for us in business and life. As in Marcus's case, he had been very successful in his pre-entrepreneurial life. He started a business with a great idea, and knew where he wanted to go. However, quickly he found himself struggling to fulfill his obligations to himself and others. And he wanted to be better – in all areas of his life, and for those he cared about.

Maybe that is where you are today: passionate about your business, but knowing that you and your life could be better. Maybe you're concerned a defined structure will inhibit your entrepreneurial spirit or creativity. But, in fact, the opposite is true. Research has shown time and again something quite different. Decision fatigue: the stress of continually making too many decisions is real. It occurs most often when we are uncertain about our role, and don't have a plan or a process to remove less important or routine tasks from our To Do list.

Whether you know it or not, you *do* have a process – humans and our brains love repetition. When examined, even in creative endeavors, there always exists a process. But following that process, a conscious, intentional one, reduces decision fatigue – which makes it easier to solve problems or be more creative. I know it sounds counter-intuitive. You become *more* effective, not less, when you have those tasks put into a process.

The other area of concern I often hear relates to the introduction of more people to the team, whether staff or contractors, and how that impacts the agility of a business. But the truth is, even in virtual businesses, very few of us can be completely separate from others. That's why a solid framework with accountability can help you achieve that goal. You create accountability for yourself by creating goals and then managing and evaluating the results. But, like Marcus had Bill, when you have someone on your team to provide mentoring, challenge your beliefs, and hold you accountable to your plan, this support structure commonly provides the most tangible success.

It's also one of the main reasons I wanted to write this book. It is heart wrenching to watch amazing, talented individuals struggle unnecessarily because they think they have to go it alone. It is your company, and ultimately, your responsibility. But deciding to take on that challenge doesn't necessarily mean you have to reinvent the wheel or climb the mountains on your own. Yes, it will be your achievement, but a guide, like a Sherpa, can add to the success of the journey, make it less dangerous, and give you confidence along the way.

Perhaps you have read many books like this one, and tried to apply the principles with less success than you had hoped. For myself, I have always wanted to write a book. But this time, I made the decision to fully commit. Every word is mine – but I had help along the way. By following a process designed by my publisher, and leveraging an editor who held me accountable, a few short months later I am finishing these last few sentences this morning. The process and the deadlines challenged me to think differently about my book and my life, and even talking out the ideas with someone who was also invested in my success made me feel more confident about what I was doing at each step.

I know it is absolutely possible to make sustainable changes, and to have the business and life you dream of. It is easier than you can imagine. If you truly decide – and I mean with your heart and soul all in – it can happen for you as well.

ACKNOWLEDGEMENTS

What to say when one of your dreams comes true? Thank you doesn't seem quite enough to everyone who helped me make this book a reality but I'm going to try.

- To my parents, Joe and Rita, who read to us before we could read ourselves, subscribed to the Book of the Month Club, and made receiving our first library card an event to celebrate, I'm eternally grateful.
- To my siblings, Rosanne, Tony, Vince, and Andria, who let me read to them and didn't mind when I turned our book collection into a library and made them check out books. I would be nowhere without you.

- To my bonus children, Tara and Jeremy, thank you for your love (and giving me the privilege of being called Nana!).

- To my friends and colleagues, and I am blessed with many, thank you for your unwavering support, believing in me when I faltered, and encouraging me to write a book. You have made my journey rich and deep.

- To the Morgan James Publishing team, David Hancock, CEO & Founder, thank you for creating the pathway to printing for this book, Megan Malone, Managing Editor, I appreciate you guiding me through the process, and of course, everyone else – Jim Howard, Bethany Marshall, Nickcole Watkins – much heartfelt thanks for helping steward this book on its journey.

- To my editors, Kate Makled and Maggie McReynolds, and the entire Difference Press Team, thank you for your guidance and for always being in the writer's corner. This has been an amazing experience.

- To Angela Lauria, Publisher, Difference Press, there are no words. I had tears when I finished your book and knew I had finally found the way to write my book. I appreciate your passion and candor more than you know. Thanks for shining a light where others have missed.

- To my husband, Russ, thank you for knowing I was going to be your wife and making sure I got the memo. Everyone should be so lucky to be in love with their number one fan.

ABOUT THE AUTHOR

 Gina Catalano is the founder of Venture Solutions, a consulting and coaching company focused on the success of small companies and their leaders. With over 20 years of experience leading and working with businesses, she has developed the *Tandem Leadership* process – an innovative strategy for entrepreneurs to work with the #2 or "second-in-command" leader in their company. She works with business leaders to achieve the results they want in all areas of their lives.

Previously, she worked as a director of consulting in addition to stints as a Vice President in entrepreneurial companies. She has been fortunate to work with some of the most dedicated professionals and amazing clients who taught her that pursuing excellence, living your passion, and enjoying your life are not mutually exclusive.

She is a Martha Beck-trained Life Coach and holds a degree in Mathematics from the University of California, Santa Barbara and a Masters of Public Administration from California State University, East Bay. She and her husband reside in southern Arizona, where they enjoy the mountains and all the desert has to offer.

Gina can either be reached at: www.gcatalano.com

Or by email at gina@venturesolutionsus.com

THANK YOU

Thank you for reading *Tandem Leadership: How Your #2 Can Make You #1.* I hope this book sparked some ideas on how to leverage the relationship between you and your key people that will provide you the results you'd like to see in your business and your life.

If you are looking to build your own *Tandem Leadership* "bicycle" for your business, please visit my website: www. TandemLeadershipBook.com. There you will find a free *Tandem Leadership* Toolkit that includes:

1. **5 Keys to Implementing Tandem Leadership** – A bonus audio on *Tandem Leadership* and how to get started.

2. **Rules of the Road** – A helpful checklist on how to avoid "flat tires" on your road to success with *Tandem Leadership.*

3. **30-Minute Strategy Session** – During this complimentary session, we will explore the opportunities and challenges you have identified in your business and what your next best step is to make your own *Tandem Leadership* journey a success.

Happy Riding!

The Morgan James
Speakers Group

www.TheMorganJamesSpeakersGroup.com

We connect Morgan James published authors with live and online events and audiences whom will benefit from their expertise.

Morgan James makes all of our titles available
through the Library for All Charity Organizations.

www.LibraryForAll.org